Tax Planning from the Heart

Tax Planning from the Heart

How to Increase Income,
Reduce Taxes,
and Help Your Favorite Charity

JOSEPH CASSELLI

as told to PAUL WINN

TEN SPEED PRESS
Berkeley, California

TEN SPEED PRESS
P.O. Box 7123
Berkeley, California 94707
www.tenspeed.com

Distributed in Australia by Simon and Schuster Australia, in Canada by Ten Speed
Press Canada, in New Zealand by Tandem Press, in South Africa by Real Books,
in Southeast Asia by Berkeley Books, and in the United Kingdom and Europe by
Airlift Books.

Cover design by Gary Bernal
Interior design by Jeff Brandenburg, ImageComp

Library of Congress Cataloging-in-Publication Data

Casselli, Joseph.
    Tax planning from the heart : a guide to creating charitable
trusts / Joseph Casselli as told to Paul Winn.
        p.   cm.
    Includes index.
    ISBN 1–58008–047–2 (alk. paper)
    1. Charitable uses, trusts, and foundations—Taxation—United
States—Popular works.   2. Estate planning—United States—Popular
works.   3. Tax planning—United States—Popular works.   I. Winn,
Paul, 1940– .   II. Title.
KF6585.C37   1998
343.7304—dc21   98–24655
                                                                                       CIP

First printing, 1998
Printed in Canada

1   2   3   4   5   6   7   8   9   10 — 02   01   00   99   98

If you are active and prosperous or young or in good health, it may be easier for you to augment your means than to diminish your wants.

But if you are wise, you will do both at the same time, young or old, rich or poor, sick or well; and if you are very wise you will do both in such a way as to augment the general happiness of society.

—Benjamin Franklin

Contents

Preface xi

Introduction: Increasing Needs and Diminishing Resources xiii
    Enabling, Not Providing—The Changing Role
        of Government xiv
    The New Self-Made American—A Matter of Necessity xv
    The Federal Government's Need for
        Revenue Enhancement xv
    Medicare, Social Security, and the Welfare System xvi
    Income Taxation xviii

CHAPTER 1: Confiscating Wealth Through Taxation 1
    Income and Estate Taxes May Take More than 70 Percent 1
    Capital Gains and Estate Taxes Take 68 Percent of a
        Company's Value 3
    How The Tax Law Operates to Confiscate Wealth 5

CHAPTER 2: The Nature of Wealth 12
    Capital 12
    Financial Capital 12
    Social Capital 13

CHAPTER 3: Trusts 14
    The Monks and Their Wine 14
    Fundamentals of Trusts 16
    Charitable Remainder Trusts 18
    Income Tax Deduction for Charitable Gifts 23
    The Unitrust and the Annuity Trust 25
    Charitable Remainder Trust—A Vehicle for Making
        Good Things Happen 34
    Other Trusts That Play a Part 34

CHAPTER 4: Uses of the Charitable Remainder Trust 36
    Tax Incentives 36
    Financial Planning Incentives 43
    Who Is Most Likely to Benefit? 46

CHAPTER 5: Increasing Retirement Income 48
    The Brewers 48
    The Lincolns 53

CHAPTER 6: Selling The Successful Business—
              Without the Tax Man 61
    The Smiths 61
    Maxwell Lyle 68

CHAPTER 7: Minimizing Estate Taxes on Substantial Estates . . 74
    The Pearsons 74

CHAPTER 8: Diversifying the Appreciated Portfolio—
              Without Taxes 81
    Joan Lerner 81

CHAPTER 9: Your Retirement Plan—A Great Way to
              Accumulate, A Terrible Way to Distribute 87
    Theresa Grant 87

CHAPTER 10: Investing Additional Spendable Income 92
    The Wilburs 92

CHAPTER 11: Avoiding Double-Dose Taxes on the
              Qualified Plans 99
    The Casses 100

CHAPTER 12: Managing the Windfall: Having Your Cake
              and Eating It, Too 106
    Benito Hernandez 106

CHAPTER 13: Where Do We Go from Here? 112

    The Need for Skilled Counsel 112

    The Kleinmans—The Danger of Going It Alone 112

    Benefits of Using a Charitable Remainder Trust 115

    The Appropriate Candidate for a

          Charitable Remainder Trust 116

    What to Expect 117

Glossary of Terms and Concepts 123

    Trust Terms and Concepts 123

    Estate Terms and Concepts 128

    Financial Terms and Concepts 130

Index 131

As I grow older, I pay less attention to what men say.
I just watch what they do.

—Andrew Carnegie

Preface

As we go to press, the ink is still drying on the Taxpayer Relief Act of 1997. This book reflects that new legislation.

Any book that intends to make a fairly complex financial subject—such as charitable tax planning—simple enough to be understood by everyone usually resorts to illustrating through example; this book is no exception to that general rule. Furthermore, whenever examples are used as vehicles for illuminating this murky financial environment, one must make assumptions—about income tax, capital gains, and estate tax rates.

Throughout this book, in the case histories presented, we have generally used a federal estate tax rate of 55 percent, although we recognize that the actual federal estate tax rate for any individual may be higher or lower. Additionally, because of the substantial differences in state law, we have ignored the impact of state inheritance and estate taxes that, if included, would further deplete the value of the estate to be passed to heirs.

Taxes on capital gains continue to be an important consideration in charitable tax planning despite the Taxpayer Relief Act's reduction in the federal capital gains tax rate for property held for twelve months or longer. The case histories presented assume a composite state and federal tax rate of 27 percent on profits resulting from the sale of appreciated property—a 20 percent federal rate and an average 7 percent state income tax rate. Since only a very few states levy no income taxes, while some have substantial rates, the 7 percent assumption seems reasonable.

The concepts and illustrations contained in the book are based on the current law as we understand it, but nothing seems so certain as change. We don't intend to or desire to practice law. The material presented is an application of general rules to individual situations. Before you act on the basis of any of these concepts, you need to consult with qualified legal, accounting, and financial counsel.

Our belief is that taxes, whether they be income, estate, or gift taxes, tend to become more onerous over time and that the temporary easing of certain taxes resulting from the Taxpayer Relief Act of 1997 is just that—temporary. Not only is the relief temporary, its effect is relatively insignificant. The danger in such legislation is that it lulls the unwary into believing their tax problems are easing. In that naive belief lie the seeds of personal financial catastrophe.

Perhaps a few books of this type are written without the help and encouragement of other people; this book isn't one of those. I owe a great deal to many people, but to attempt to list them all would result, inevitably, in forgetting someone. So, I won't attempt it. Instead, let me just say thank you to my friends at Renaissance, Inc., for their support and promotion of philanthropy, and to Lee Hoffman, president of PhilanthroTec, Inc., for his marvelously informative *Harnessing the Power of the Charitable Remainder Trust.* I want to thank Terry Kendall, former chief executive of Golden American Life Insurance Company and now senior vice president of Life, Accident, Health and Pension of Cigna International for his friendship, help, and guidance.

To my children: Michele, Steve, and Jennifer who will be forever a gift of enduring pride. Finally, to my wife and companion, Evelyn, whose support and encouragement are unconditional.

Introduction: Increasing Needs and Diminishing Resources

A generous man will himself be blessed,
For he shares his food with the poor.

—Proverbs 22:9

. . . IT IS POSSIBLE THAT IN THE TWENTY-FIRST CENTURY A LIFE SPAN EXCEEDING 100 YEARS MAY BE COMMONPLACE.

The average American living when the nineteenth century became the twentieth could expect to live about forty-seven years. By the year 2000, the average life expectancy will be almost 80 years, and it is possible that in the twenty-first century a life span exceeding 100 years may be commonplace. Humanity's genius in eradicating the illnesses that plague us means that our lives can be longer—maybe substantially longer. But are we willing to pay the price in quality for what we are achieving in quantity? In simpler words, our lives may be longer, but will they be better? Are they even as good as they were? Let's consider a study by the U.S. Department of Health and Human Services.

To the extent that "better" can be equated with at least adequate material well-being, the study is eye opening. According to the study, of 100 people starting their careers at age twenty-five, here is what happened by the time they reached—or would have reached—age sixty-five.

- 25 were dead

- 15 had incomes of less than $4,800

- 56 had a median income of about $7,200

- 4 had incomes in excess of $31,000

The income numbers sound like they might have come from the 1930s; in fact, they reflect the situation in the late 1980s.

Enabling Not Providing— The Changing Role of Government

There is evidence that Social Security is sick and getting sicker. It is estimated that by the year 2011, more benefits will be paid out than deposits taken in, and the Social Security trust fund surplus will be wiped out. There are 3.2 workers making payments into the Social Security system today for each Social Security recipient. By the year 2029, each recipient will be supported by only 2.1 workers making payments into the system. That's a reduction of 34 percent.

Medicare, that monster program appended to the Social Security system, will be out of money to pay the hospital bills for Medicare recipients by the year 2000 at the current projections, yet, it is estimated that a man aged sixty-five in 2011 may pay nearly $115,000 in health and long-term care costs during retirement, and a woman will pay about 10 percent more.

Government's answer to these problems has been largely to offer incentives to Americans to provide for themselves. Some of the answers have been

- Increasing the spousal IRA from $250 to $2,000

- Experimenting with Medical Savings Accounts

- Authorizing SIMPLEs

- Developing a pilot program to shift Medicare to HMOs

The message from Uncle Sam is clear. With existing social programs in serious economic danger, increased taxes will be needed just to keep the current safety nets repaired. For the economic wherewithal to meet the greater needs occasioned by an enhanced mortality, Americans will have to provide for themselves.

The New Self-Made American—A Matter of Necessity

INSTEAD OF BEING PROTECTED AND PROVIDED FOR, THE CITIZEN IS "ENABLED" AND "EMPOWERED."

> America's safety nets are in disrepair. The cradle-to-grave American employer has become extinct. The individual economic dislocation that is an unfortunate part of the corporate need to seek ever-higher profits will strain the safety nets even further. The vision of economic safety and prosperity that began with the New Deal and was buoyed by the Great Society has been shattered by the cold reality of global economics. The age of the new self-made American may be at hand. Instead of being protected and provided for, the citizen is "enabled" and "empowered." If the new American is to be self-made, it is because it's a matter of necessity.

For Americans it's a call to arms. First, we need to recognize that our future well-being and that of our families will require an increasing financial sophistication, a measure of which will be offered in the pages that follow. Second, if we acknowledge humanity's fundamental duty to care for those among us who are hungry or homeless or damaged, we need to be aware of the available opportunities to provide that assistance in a way that gives them the greatest benefit. The following pages will point a way to accomplishing that, as well. Third, we need to understand that the burden of income taxes will make the first two objectives more difficult.

The Federal Government's Need for Revenue Enhancement

In 1993, the Clinton administration embarked on an initiative called the National Performance Review (NPR) designed to make the federal government leaner and more responsive. Known as "reinventing government," the project's goal was a saving of $108 billion over five years. Almost immediately, the Congress voted to exempt the Veteran's Health Administration, which makes up approximately 10 percent of the federal workforce, and all of the federal criminal justice employees. Additionally, the administration's proposal to merge the Federal Bureau of Investigation and the Drug Enforcement Administration has been shelved.[1]

---

[1] "Twelve Months Wiser: Reinventing Government." *The Economist,* September 17, 1994, p. 26.

The federal civilian payroll growth slowed to an average 1.72 percent in the two-year period of 1994–95 from a 6.44 average annual growth in the preceding twenty-three years. While the 1996 federal employment numbers continue to show a slowing of the growth of the federal government, it is unlikely that the savings realized will come close to the $108 billion goal. Even if we were fortunate enough to realize all of the goal, there are a number of factors that strongly indicate that government's need for revenue will grow; in fact, it can be expected to grow significantly. The result is likely to be—despite the 1997 reduction in certain taxes—an overall growth in taxes.

Medicare, Social Security, and the Welfare System

An early 1997 headline screams:

President Warns that Social Security System Could Go Belly Up.

The American public has been warned repeatedly that, at the current rate of benefit entitlement, the Social Security system will run out of money during the lifetime of most of you reading these words. Let's consider the issues and their likely effect upon tax rates.

Of all Americans over age sixty-five, 87 percent have annual incomes of less than $25,000. Looked at even more closely, we would find that a large percentage live at or below the federal poverty level.

There are currently about 63,000 Americans aged 100 or older. What was once an oddity—reaching age 100—is becoming more common-place. By the year 2030, it is estimated that the number of centenarians in the United States will exceed 360,000.

Life expectancy has increased by **almost 70 percent** since 1900. By the year 2000, the average life expectancy will be 78.8 years. The fastest-growing population segment in America is comprised of people over age eighty-five.

FOR SOCIAL SECURITY ALONE, THE "UNFUNDED LIABILITY . . ."
IS ESTIMATED AT MORE THAN $7 TRILLION.

> The Social Security system, unlike a legal reserve insurance system, operates on a pay-as-you-go basis. Benefits paid to current Social Security recipients are being supported by currently-employed citizens paying into the system.

Today, with 144 million workers supporting 50 million Americans receiving Social Security benefits, there are approximately 2.9 workers for each Social Security recipient. By the year 2029, the number of recipients will have increased to the point where only two workers will be available to support each recipient. Elizabeth Kolbert, in her 1995 *New York Times* magazine article, cites an earlier article by Paul Samuelson in which he declares Social Security to be actuarially unsound and compares it to the greatest Ponzi game ever contrived.[2] Kolbert further observes that "even in the current debate over cutting Medicare, both sides [Republicans and Democrats] have effectively conspired to obscure the truth about the issue...."[3]

The truth about the issue, as Kolbert sees it, is that "For Social Security alone, the 'unfunded liability'—the difference between the benefits the government expects to pay out and the taxes it expects to take in—is estimated at more than $7 trillion."[4]

It seems clear that the Social Security system, in its present form, is in serious trouble. Susan Dentzer, in a recent *U.S. News & World Report* article, stated, "Unless you live under a rock, you know that Social Security's long-range future looks bleak."[5]

An obvious means of beginning to remedy the trouble is to pare the benefits provided by the system—yet, this hasn't been done on any substantial basis. The reason for this inaction lies in two areas. First, there is the moral imperative of government's making good on the system's promises. For the more cynical, there is the fact that Social Security recipients comprise the largest and fastest growing voting block. That political clout would appear to ensure that benefits are unlikely to undergo significant cuts. But what is the answer?

The answer is likely to be increased taxation. And it is just this taxation that will make it more difficult to accumulate the personal wealth needed to avoid the over-reliance on the Social Security system.

---

[2] Who Will Face the Music?" Elizabeth Kolbert. *The New York Times Magazine,* August 27, 1965, p. 56.

[3] *ibid.*

[4] *ibid.*

[5] "Social Security: Hot Summer Sequel." Susan Dentzer. *U.S. News & World Report,* July 8, 1996, p. 49.

". . . THE MEDICARE TAB WILL . . . DEVOUR 18 PERCENT OF THE FEDERAL BUDGET—MORE THAN THE GOVERNMENT NOW SPENDS ON EDUCATION, CRIME, AND DEFENSE COMBINED."

It is likely that Medicare will have a similar effect on future tax rates. It has been estimated that 90 percent of a person's expenditure on health care occurs in the last 1 percent of his life, but the Medicare Hospital Insurance Trust Fund may be out of money to pay the hospital bills for senior citizens and disabled Americans by the year 2000. In fact, ". . . the Congressional Budget Office estimates that the Medicare tab will reach $463 billion a year by 2006 and devour 18 percent of the federal budget—more than the government now spends on education, crime, and defense combined."[6] Just as we noted that Social Security will not be permitted to fail and, in fact, will be bailed out by additional taxes, so will Medicare.

Income Taxation

It is almost impossible to believe—income taxes having become a staple of our financial diet—but the 1913 composition of income taxes was for less than 10 percent and was promised to be temporary! This once-temporary levy, which helped finance World War I, has become a major obstacle to the accumulation of wealth. We need only compare the differences in accumulating money in a non-taxed environment with that of a normally taxed savings or investment plan. There is no question about the dampening effect of taxes.

For example, let's compare the growth of an investment of $10,000 at an 8 percent interest rate in a no-tax environment with the same investment and growth rate at a 39.6 percent marginal income tax rate.

---

[6] "Here's How We Will Reform Medicare and Social Security Beginning in 1997." Ann Reilly Dowd, *Money,* Winter 1996, p. 19.

INVESTMENT PERIOD	AFTER-TAX INVESTMENT BALANCE AT 39.6% INCOME TAX RATE	AFTER-TAX INVESTMENT BALANCE AT 0% INCOME TAX RATE	PERCENTAGE LOST DUE TO INCOME TAXES
5 Years	$12,661	$14,693	$13.8%
10 Years	$16,080	$21,589	25.7%
15 Years	$20,296	$31,722	36.0%
20 Years	$25,697	$46,610	44.9%
25 Years	$32,535	$68,485	52.5%
30 Years	$41,192	$100,000	59.1%

The important issue, of course, is not where tax rates have been. It is where tax rates are likely to go from here. With an eye to developing an intuitive sense of future tax rate movement, let's take a look at the top marginal tax rates in effect since the income tax was imposed and examine some of the current issues that are likely to affect future tax rates. Once we have a sense of the movement of taxes—even if we can only imagine the details—we can begin to create a strategy for dealing with them.

IT [THE IMPORTANT ISSUE] IS WHERE TAX RATES ARE LIKELY TO GO FROM HERE.

Early top marginal income tax rates rose every few years after their 1913 imposition until they reached their early peak of 65% in 1922. Beginning in 1924, they declined gradually to 20 percent and remained at that level from 1928 through 1932. This was their lowest period since WWI— and they were more than double the level at which they were initially imposed. In 1933, the top marginal income tax rates again jumped, this time to 55 percent, and they have remained at 50% or greater—exceeding 90 percent during the latter years of WWII—until 1987 when they declined to 28 percent for a four-year period.

It is important to understand that just as the first tax-rate low was more than double the 1913 level, the second low was almost triple the 1913 level. Since 1990, the top marginal tax rate has increased every few years and, in 1997, was almost 40 percent. Again, looked at graphically, the history of the marginal income rates has been a series of peaks and valleys—*but each peak and valley was higher than the earlier ones.*

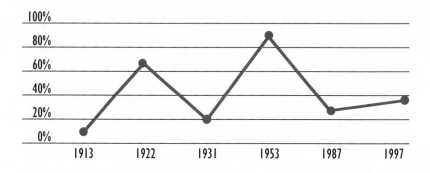

Now that we have looked at some of society's sacred cows, let's think, for a moment, about where future income tax rates are likely to go.

Historically, personal income tax rates have trended higher. Each peak has been higher than the previous peak, and each valley higher than the previous one. Without substantial and immediate remedies, Social Security may be bankrupt. The Medicare trustees believe that ensuring the program's solvency will be painful. Balance those needs and that tax history with the political savvy and power of the over-age sixty-five voting block who cast fear into the hearts of legislators. It simply isn't reasonable to believe that, in the long term, taxes will be anything other than higher and more onerous. The alternative would be an almost draconian cut in benefits and, politically, that is suicide.

There is a story about a frog and a scorpion. It seems that during an unexpected flood, a scorpion was in danger of drowning. Being unable to swim, the scorpion approached a frog and asked if he could climb on the frog's back while the frog swam to safety. The frog said that he was concerned the scorpion would sting him. The scorpion pointed out that if the frog permitted him to climb aboard his back and the scorpion stung him they would both die—the frog from the sting and the scorpion from drowning. The frog acknowledged that the argument made sense and he allowed the scorpion to climb onto his back. As the frog swam across the rising water, the scorpion stung him. In pain and realizing the end was near, the frog turned his head and, staring at the scorpion, asked him why he had stung him. The scorpion responded that it was nothing personal; it was just his nature.

Just as it is in the nature of the scorpion to sting, it is in the nature of government to tax. There will be—and have been—temporary reductions in one or more taxes, often motivated by the "wet finger in the air" system of government. They are, necessarily, temporary. The trend—indeed the almost inexorable line of future tax—is up. History suggests that, even without the impetus of the needed repair of tattered social safety nets, government levies tend to become greater over time. But, coupled with the need to mend the social fabric, can the trend line of future taxes be anything but inclined? We don't know for sure, of course. But, the indicators of future, onerous taxes—despite the recent Taxpayer Relief Act—seem to be strong indeed.

This book is intended to help you weather that tax storm on the horizon. It will introduce you to a number of clients—really composites of various clients—who have chosen a tax-wise method of achieving their financial goals and providing, very generously, for those charitable organizations that mean the most to them. You will learn, in detail, how these clients avoided the tax man; it is legal, smart, and encouraged by the government.

1 Confiscating Wealth Through Taxation

It is important to realize the negative effects of taxation. In our introduction to this book, we even showed that, over a thirty-year period, an income tax rate of 39.6 percent resulted in a loss of more than 59 percent of an investment. Tables and graphs, however, aren't as convincing as are stories about people like you and me whose encounters with the tax system left them angry, disillusioned, and poorer. We are going to look at only two examples—and there are many—of how taxes can be devastating.

Income and Estate Taxes
May Take More than 70 Percent

Bill and Sharon Coffey had owned and operated a successful advertising business for thirty years, when they retired at Bill's age sixty-five, seventeen years ago. The company had instituted a pension plan in the early years of the business, and, throughout his business life, Bill had seen his pension account grow from year to year. When Bill retired, his vested account amounted to just over $2 million. Since the sale of the company entailed an annual payment to Bill and Sharon that provided sufficient income to meet their needs, both Bill and Sharon rolled their account balances into rollover IRAs and allowed them to continue to accumulate on a tax-deferred basis to provide a substantial inheritance to Lori and Dan, their children.

... THE $3 MILLION IRA INHERITANCE HAD SHRUNK TO LESS THAN $816,000.

> Sharon and Bill died just months apart, and when Bill died, his IRA had grown to just over $3 million. After meeting with the estate's attorney and accountant, Dan and Lori

discovered that the $3 million IRA inheritance had shrunk to less than $816,000 as a result of a combination of income taxes their father had never paid on his pension fund and estate taxes. The estate taxes, at 55 percent, took a substantial portion of the inheritance.

ESTATE ANALYSIS

IRA assets in taxable estate	$3,002,023
Estate tax rate	✕ 55%
Estate tax payable on IRA assets	$1,651,113

There would be additional costs for state inheritance taxes and probate costs, but we should discuss the federal taxes first. If you look at the next estate analysis, you will see the abbreviation *IRD*. This means "income in respect of a decedent."

ESTATE ANALYSIS

IRA assets in gross estate	$3,002,023
Estate tax payable	− 1,651,113
IRD	$1,350,910
Income tax rate	✕ 39.6%
Income tax payable	$ 534,960

The income in respect of a decedent is the amount that remains of an IRA that wasn't taken in federal estate taxes. Since Dan and Lori's father had never paid income taxes on that money, the income taxes had to be paid now, and they amounted to more than $500,000.

The separate tax items add up thus:

Federal estate taxes	$1,651,113
Federal income taxes	$ 534,960
Total taxes on the IRA	$2,186,073

HOW HAD SUCH WONDERFUL PARENTS CREATED SUCH A MESS!

The total federal taxes on the IRA amount to 72.82 percent of the individual retirement account value. The $3,000,000 inheritance that the Coffeys had planned to leave their children amounted to less than 30 percent of that amount; taxes had consumed the rest of it. Furthermore, the state is likely to claim some of its own income taxes and inheritance taxes. How had such wonderful parents created such a mess! The 45 percent of the IRA that was not consumed by federal estate taxes was subject to a 39.6 percent federal income tax. If we represent the distribution of the IRA graphically, it looks like this:

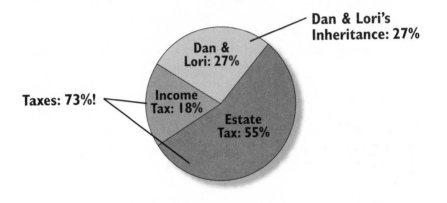

Lori and Dan agreed, after looking at the graph, that there had to be a better way to arrange for a secure retirement than the tax disaster their parents left.

Capital Gains and Estate Taxes Take 68 percent of a Company's Value

Over a period of thirty years, Max Kirtland had seen his printing business grow from a small mom-and-pop shop to a thriving specialty publishing house with eighty employees. He and his wife, Nancy, tended the growing business over the years, weathering changes and problems that, Max had admitted, would have made him decide to sell the business if it hadn't been for Nancy's help and encouragement.

Max and Nancy had been so involved in the business that their sons, Ken and Max junior, seemed to have grown up almost by themselves. When Nancy and Max had time to think about it, they were saddened by the realization that they had missed much of their children's childhood. Now that the two of them had three grandchildren, they vowed not to let that happen a second time.

Three years ago, they sold the business to a competing publishing house for $5 million, determined to enjoy their grandchildren's childhood in a way they had never enjoyed their own sons'. Taxes had been a problem, but they expected them; that was the price they paid to get the equity out of the business. Since most of the growth their company had enjoyed was due to their own efforts and most of their costs had been depreciated, Max and Nancy had almost no remaining cost basis at the time of the sale (cost basis, for our purposes, being the total investment in the company less any depreciation taken). Any remaining cost basis that Max and Nancy had would offset the sale price of the business and reduce the taxes payable. As a result, their state income and federal capital gains tax amounted to $1,350,000, leaving them $3,650,000 to invest in order to produce their annual income. Nancy died last year, and Max only two months ago.

ALMOST $3.4 MILLION WAS PAID IN TAXES ON A $5 MILLION ASSET!

Ken and Junior had been told that their parents sold the company for $5 million and were surprised that only $3,650,000 was left. They learned from the executor of their father's estate that, when the federal estate taxes were paid on the remaining proceeds, the amount remaining from the $5 million company would be $1,642,500; more than $2 million in federal estate taxes would need to be paid on that money. In total, almost $3,400,000 was paid in taxes on a $5 million asset!

How the Tax Law Operates to Confiscate Wealth

Not only is the imposition of taxes the way governments fund their operations—including paying for standing armies, wars, foreign aid, and feeding the poor—taxes are also a means of bringing about a result the government feels is "desirable." Estate tax is a perfect example of this latter objective.

Much of United States law comes from the common law, the body of law developed in England and constituting the basis of the English and U.S. legal systems. Over the centuries, the English property ownership system that developed was, largely, feudal; vast property ownership was concentrated in the hands of a relatively few families who, in addition to their property ownership, enjoyed other considerable wealth. In large part, their property was a gift from the ruling monarch who demanded, in return, that the property owner be available to fight the monarch's battles. Over time—and with the development of a monetary system—the enterprising property owner hired mercenaries to fulfill his obligation to the monarch or, simply, paid a tax.

Arising out of this system were, essentially, two social and economic classes: landed gentry and peasants. Eventually, these classes became defined as an upper class landed society and a lower class. While the perquisites enjoyed by the upper class were always significantly greater than those available to the lower class, the difference in quality of life eventually took on a Dickensian quality, as property became ever more concentrated in the hands of the few. The English system of primogeniture, providing an exclusive right of inheritance to the eldest son, further concentrated these holdings.

In an effort to break up the concentration of property—as well as to fatten the Exchequer—a system of inheritance taxation was introduced. The result for many families, often land rich but cash poor, was the sale of some or all of their ancestral land. With considerable modification, of course, this system continues in the United States and is the basis of estate taxes.

Estate Taxes

Any tax that may take up to 55 percent of your assets deserves your full and complete attention. The place to begin to understand how an estate tax works is to understand just what assets are taxed. We need to start by determining what makes up a person's *gross estate.* The easy answer is that the gross estate includes everything that you own—or have any incidents of ownership in—at the time of your death, along with a few things that you thought you had given away before you died. To more fully understand, however, we need to dig deeper. Let's take a look at the property that constitutes the gross estate.

The gross estate, for federal estate tax purposes, includes, but isn't limited to

- **ANY PROPERTY YOU OWN AT DEATH**—This includes your house, furnishings, jewelry, stocks, bonds, mutual funds, mortgages, notes, and personal effects. Your share of any property that you own in concert with others is also included, such as property that you hold as tenant in common. Your right to future commissions, royalties, or rents also constitute property you own.

- **YOUR LIFE INSURANCE**—Perhaps the most startling revelation to many people when they begin to think about estate taxes is that the death benefit of life insurance owned by them at death is included in their estate for tax purposes. Your death benefit may not be distributed by your probate estate (i.e., by your will)—in fact, it usually is not—but if you owned the life insurance when you died, its value balloons your estate. (We will look at some very effective methods of dealing with this problem later.) Furthermore, even if you did not own the policy, but it was payable to or for the benefit of your estate, it will be considered a part of it.

- **CERTAIN PROPERTY TRANSFERRED BY YOU WITHIN THREE YEARS OF DEATH**—Believe it or not, even though you give certain property away, for example, you make a gift of it to your children, it may still be considered a part of your estate. The principal asset in this category is life insurance. Many people who may not have had the time or inclination to plan for the minimizing of their taxes find, late in life, that the life insurance that they own may only be worth 45 percent of its death benefit because 55 percent of it will be lost in estate taxes. In an attempt to remedy that, they might transfer ownership to their children or to an irrevocable trust. If they fail to survive at least three years from the transfer, the gift of life insurance will be deemed to have been made *in contemplation of death* and will be considered a part of the estate—even though the insured no longer had any ownership.

- **CERTAIN PROPERTY TRANSFERRED BY YOU IN WHICH YOU RETAINED SOME INTEREST**—For example, if you transferred your life insurance policy to your children but retained the right to receive dividends from the policy or the right to change the beneficiary, the life insurance will be considered to be a part of your estate, even if the transfer was made more than three years ago. If you owned the controlling interest in your company and transferred it to an irrevocable trust while retaining the right to the income produced by the shares, your retaining of that right to income would be enough to cause the entire value of the shares to be considered a part of your estate. Another example of gifted property included in your estate is property in which you retained a life estate. A house that you had given to your daughter, but in which you kept the right to reside for the balance of your life, would be considered part of your estate.

When all of these assets are identified and valued, the total value is called the *gross estate*. Estate taxes—which, as we have already seen, can be very onerous—are still several steps away. Let's move on to the next step that the executor will usually take—determining the *adjusted gross estate*.

Once all of the assets that need to be included in the estate are determined and a total value is arrived at, certain deductions need to be taken to arrive at the adjusted gross estate. Those deductions are

- **FUNERAL EXPENSES**—Funeral expenses are generally limited to a reasonable amount and include the cost of a headstone, embalming, burial lot, interment, and transportation to the cemetery.

- **ADMINISTRATIVE EXPENSES**—These are the fees of the various professionals who provide services to the estate and include attorneys' and accountants' fees, executor's commissions, appraisal fees and brokerage costs, as well as court costs and the expenses incurred in collecting and preserving the assets and paying estate debts.

- **DEBTS**—These include mortgages and certain taxes, such as unpaid income, gift, and property taxes that had accrued prior to death, as well as other debts for which you are personally liable.

- **THEFT AND CASUALTY LOSSES**—To be deductible, the loss must have occurred during the time the estate was in the process of being settled and before it was closed. These are losses caused by fire, storms, shipwreck (or other casualty), or by theft.

Once these deductions have been taken—deductions that represent "costs" to the estate—we arrive at the *adjusted gross estate*. Arriving at the *taxable estate* is just a deduction—actually two deductions—away.

From the adjusted gross estate, the executor will deduct two amounts to determine the amount of the taxable estate:

- **MARITAL DEDUCTION**—This is the amount that passes to a spouse. Under the current law, *everything* included in the gross estate on which ownership passes to a surviving spouse is deductible under the marital deduction provision. While a strategy that calls for all assets to be passed to a surviving spouse would seem to be the best one, since it avoids the estate tax, the result of that strategy is often just a delaying of the problem, since those assets will be taxed when the surviving spouse eventually dies. The second problem with such a strategy is that the unified credit ($192,800 in 1997 and increasing gradually to $345,800 by 2006) to which the estate of each spouse is entitled would be lost to the first spouse's estate, because the credit is against estate taxes owed; since no tax would be owed by the estate if all of the assets were passed to a spouse, the credit would remain unused. We will address this issue later in our discussion.

- **CHARITABLE DEDUCTION**—This is the amount passed to a "qualified charity" at death. The limit on the amount of deduction is equal to the value of the property included in the gross estate. So, if all of the assets included in the estate were left to a charity, the estate would deduct the entire amount of the estate.

Once the total of these two deductions is subtracted from the adjusted gross estate, we are left with the taxable estate. We need to add the total of adjusted taxable gifts to this amount to arrive at the amount on which estate taxes are based. These adjusted taxable gifts are the total of the taxable portions of any gifts made since 1976.[7] The resulting sum is called the *tentative tax base*.

---

[7] In a general sense, a gift is taxable to the extent that it is greater than (a) the annual gift tax exclusion or (b) the gift tax charitable deduction.

The progressive estate tax rates are applied to the amount of assets constituting the tentative tax base. These estate tax rates are as shown below.

ESTATE TAX

| IF TAXABLE ESTATE IS: | | THE TENTATIVE ESTATE TAX IS: | | |
OVER	BUT NOT OVER	$	PLUS %	OVER
	$10,000		18%	
$10,000	$20,000	$1,800	20%	$10,000
$20,000	$40,000	$3,800	22%	$20,000
$40,000	$60,000	$8,200	24%	$40,000
$60,000	$80,000	$13,000	26%	$60,000
$80,000	$100,000	$18,200	28%	$80,000
$100,000	$150,000	$23,800	30%	$100,000
$150,000	$250,000	$38,800	32%	$150,000
$250,000	$500,000	$70,800	34%	$250,000
$500,000	$750,000	$155,800	37%	$500,000
$750,000	$1,000,000	$248,300	39%	$750,000
$1,000,000	$1,250,000	$345,800	41%	$1,000,000
$1,250,000	$1,500,000	$448,300	43%	$1,250,000
$1,500,000	$2,000,000	$555,800	45%	$1,500,000
$2,000,000	$2,500,000	$780,800	49%	$2,000,000
$2,500,000	$3,000,000	$1,025,800	53%	$2,500,000
$3,000,000		$1,290,800	55%	$3,000,000

As an example, let's assume you have a tentative tax base of $4 million, which is made up of everything you own. The tentative federal estate tax is calculated as follows:

Tentative tax base	$4,000,000	
Tentative tax on first	− 3,000,000	$1,290,800
Tentative tax on excess	$1,000,000	+ 550,000
Total tentative tax		$1,840,800

Earlier, when we were discussing the marital deduction, I alluded to a tax credit that could be lost. That *unified tax credit* is a credit against any federal estate taxes due and is available to all estates to the extent that federal estate taxes are payable up to the amount phased in at the time of death. The credit amount was $192,800 in 1997 and will be increased each year through 2006, at which time it will be completely phased in at $345,800. Once the tentative tax amount has been calculated, there are four credits that may be applied to that tax:

- **UNIFIED CREDIT**—This is a tax credit of between $192,800 and $345,800 (depending upon the date of death) available to everyone; however, if no federal estate tax is payable, the credit is lost. The year by year phase in is as follows:

YEAR	UNIFIED CREDIT	SHELTERED AMOUNT
1997	$192,800	$ 600,000
1998	202,050	625,000
1999	211,300	650,000
2000	220,550	675,000
2001	220,550	675,000
2002	229,800	700,000
2003	229,800	700,000
2004	287,300	850,000
2005	326,300	950,000
2006	345,800	1,000,000

- **STATE DEATH TAX CREDIT**—This tax credit is equal to the lesser of the actual state death tax paid and the amount in the maximum credit table.

- **FOREIGN DEATH TAX CREDIT**—This tax credit is equal to the death taxes paid to a foreign country or a U.S. possession on property that is situated in that country but included in the individual's gross estate.

- **TAXES ON PRIOR TRANSFERS CREDIT**—This is a diminishing credit for transfer taxes previously paid on property transferred to the individual within the last ten years; the tax credit is equal to 100 percent of the federal estate tax paid on that property, reducing by 20 percent every two years until it ceases in ten years.

Let's return to our calculation. Assuming there were no prior transfer credits or foreign tax credits and you had no property situated in a state that levied state death taxes, our only credit would be the unified tax credit. The tax due on your estate with a tentative tax base of $4 million if you died in 1998 would be $1,638,000.

FEDERAL ESTATE TAX DUE

(Death in 1998)

Tentative tax	$1,840,800
Unified tax credit	− 202,050
Estate tax due	$1,638,750

Of All Sad Words by Tongue or Pen . . .

We have looked at Bill and Sharon Coffey and Max Kirtland and seen a $3 million asset reduced to about $800,000 and $3.4 million paid in taxes on a $5 million asset. When I think about Bill and Sharon and Max, I am reminded of the hopelessness contained in the words of Will and Ariel Durant, who wrote:

Of all sad words by tongue or pen,
the saddest are these: 'It might have been.'

In the cases of Bill and Sharon and Max, their estates need not have been left as they were. There are techniques and tools that could have saved millions of dollars—and which are, in fact, saving millions each day. That is what this book is all about.

2 The Nature of Wealth

A generous man will prosper;
He who refreshes others will
Himself be refreshed.

—Proverbs 11:25

Capital

In common parlance, when we talk about capital we are really describing assets. Although business normally defines capital as the sum total of productive resources used by a firm to produce a product for sale, for most of us *capital* is a far less rigidly defined term. It is what we own—or what we think we own.

We saw earlier, in the case of the Coffeys and Max Kirtland, that much of what they thought they owned really wasn't theirs at all. It was destined to be returned to the government in taxes. In the case of the Coffeys, those taxes confiscated more than 70 percent of what they considered their capital. In light of that, we might want to characterize capital as being of two types: the wealth that we keep and the wealth that we can't keep. For now, let's label these two types of capital *financial capital* and *social capital*, respectively.

Financial Capital

The wealth that we keep, spend, or pass to our heirs is *financial capital.* As we have already seen—and as we will see again and again in this book as we look into the lives of others—for many, financial capital represents less than half of our total wealth.

In large measure, our job is to increase that financial capital by reducing the amount of wealth that we can't keep. Inevitably, as long as there exists significant wealth in the hands of individuals, this wealth erosion will be an issue. Interestingly, few people realize that the taxes that are levied—and which are the basis of this erosion—are, in reality, only an option. The U.S. government gives us another option.

Social Capital

Social capital is so called because of its eventual use. By law, it is destined to fund social programs—to feed a hungry child, imprison a felon, pay a farmer not to produce tobacco, to build a missile to defend our country. For most of us, our social capital is represented by the taxes that we pay. Let's call this *involuntary* social capital. To the extent that it is involuntary, we have no control over its use.

The option that our government provides allows us to change that *involuntary* social capital—over whose use we have no control—into *voluntary* social capital—over which we have a great deal of control! We can support the country's general welfare indirectly, through estate and capital gains taxes, or directly, through gifts to charity. For someone who has concerns about his or her support becoming foreign aid used to arm a subsequently belligerent nation or to provide price supports for commodities, like tobacco, that kill and cripple, the option to direct one's social capital has enormous appeal.

We need only look at the federal budget to realize that we have little understanding or control of how our wealth is used when taxes consume our social capital. This option allows us to turn our tax dollars, spent at the government's discretion, into charitable gifts made to organizations of our choice and over which we have control. It is interesting to note that once people understand the concept of social capital, they choose the alternative that gives them control—even before they realize it is in their financial interest to do it. How serendipitous that what we might choose on moral or social grounds also makes sense on financial grounds.

3 Trusts

The Monks and Their Wine

Often the most complex concepts begin with the simplest ideas; the concept of the trust is no different. The need that the first trust was designed to fill was straightforward. Specifically, there was a need to separate the "interests" that were conferred by the simple fact of property ownership. These interests might best be characterized as (a) ownership and (b) use. Two stories come down to us from the Middle Ages. Either or both may be apocryphal, but they illustrate the idea wonderfully. The first story is about the monks and their wine.

Legend has it that there existed a monastery whose monks were well known for both their wine-making ability and their prodigious capacity to consume it. As their wine-making reputation spread throughout Europe, the fortunes of the monastery grew. It wasn't long before this wealth became something of an embarrassment to church leaders, who suggested to the abbot that this prosperity may have been inconsistent with the monks' vow of poverty. The abbot was said to have replied that they were not at all interested in the wealth their skill conferred but, rather, their interest lay in the making and drinking of wine. In fact, they were not interested in owning it at all, only in its use. Just that quickly, a need was born.

As the storehouse of knowledge in the Middle Ages, the church was probably best equipped to resolve this problem. After sharpening their reasoning skills by determining the largest number of angels that could dance on the head of a pin, creating a way to solve this somewhat more practical problem was almost easy. The solution lay in creating a fictional entity that split the concept of ownership into two pieces: current use and residual ownership. That fictional entity was the first living trust. Under that solution, the trust would own the wine and the wealth it created, while the monks, happily led by the abbot, contented themselves with

14

making and drinking wine. Since the monastery owned no part of the wealth or the wine-making process, the monks' vow of poverty remained inviolate, and their thirst continued to be quenched.

Our second story also takes us back to the Middle Ages, and to the feudal system under which kings granted parcels of land known as *fiefs* to loyal followers in return for their agreement to fight the king's battles. With the development of a monetary system in Europe, this agreement to bear arms in the king's interest was gradually replaced by the payment of a fee to the king. This fee enabled the king to staff a mercenary army rather than rely on an aging group of knights. It seemed to be a "win–win" situation. The knights avoided all that bloodshed, and the king raised a more experienced, expert, and professional military force.

As with most taxes, however, this fee eventually came to be seen as a burdensome intrusion on the otherwise pleasant existence of the landed gentry. As such, it was a problem requiring a solution. The fee paid to the king was in return for their continued ownership of the land the king had granted them. A solution that was really no solution was to return the land to the king. While returning the land would eliminate the tax, the obviously unpalatable result of giving up their social station needed to be avoided. Since the tax followed the ownership of the land, the question became one of determining how the knight could give away the ownership but continue to use the land. Furthermore, the person to whom the land was given would be expected to pay the king. Since he would have to pay, wouldn't he also demand to use the land? As history found in the case of the monks and their wine, the solution again revolved about the medieval church.

The church in the Middle Ages—not unlike the church today—could own property without being required to pay a fee to the king. It was not long before someone (possibly one of the churchmen) realized the situation was pregnant with possibilities. Since church property was exempt from the tax, the knights' transfer of their property to the church would cause the fees normally paid on that property to cease. It was a solution in search of a problem. If the knights would trust the churchmen to keep their promise of allowing the knights continued use of the land in return for the land's transfer to the church, everyone—with the significant exception of the king—would benefit. The church obtained title, and the knight continued to use the land but paid no fees for it. So, the first trust was created.

It doesn't really matter which version you believe; both may be fiction. What does matter is that a powerful tool for producing a desirable outcome was created. This tool has since evolved significantly into one of considerable flexibility and commensurate complexity. While a full understanding of trust design and capabilities is unnecessarily time consuming and burdensome for most people, an understanding of trust fundamentals can go a long way towards raising everyone's comfort level with this key to wealth preservation on the one hand, and a kinder, gentler society on the other.

Fundamentals of Trusts

Perhaps the easiest way to envision a trust is to see it as a relationship created by and in the form of a written document. This relationship divides the ownership of property, which has been transferred to the trust into two pieces: legal title and beneficial interest. The legal title is held by the trustee (more about trustees later), and the beneficial interest is owned by the beneficiaries of the trust.

Trusts can be categorized along various dimensions: whether they can be changed or not, whether they are established during a person's life or only upon his or her death, and in many other ways.

Revocable and Irrevocable Trusts

One of the most fundamental distinctions between trusts has to do with the creator's (i.e., the grantor's) ability to change or cancel the trust once it has been established. A *revocable* trust is one in which the grantor has retained the right to change or cancel the trust during his or her lifetime. In contrast, an *irrevocable* trust is one in which the grantor has given up the power to change or cancel the trust.

A question will form in the mind of most people after reading the difference between the trusts. Specifically, why would anyone want to give up their right to change or cancel something as significant as a trust? The answer is simple: Important benefits can be gained by creating an irrevocable trust that are not available in a revocable trust. The two most important benefits of an irrevocable trust, for the purposes of this book, are

- Assets placed in an irrevocable trust are not subject to estate taxation upon the grantor's death.[8]

- Gifts of assets to an irrevocable trust are considered to be completed gifts and will, therefore, qualify for income tax deductions if made to a qualified charity.

---

[8] The exception to this relates to the *causa mortis* rule, which causes life insurance transferred within three years of death to be considered as being made in contemplation of death and, therefore, becomes a part of the decedent's estate for tax purposes.

In simpler terms, the use of the irrevocable trust, as described in this book, will, if properly drawn for a suitable client, result in substantial income tax and estate tax savings. Depending upon the particular situation in which the trusts (there are often more than one required) are used, the savings could amount to millions of dollars.

Inter Vivos and Testamentary Trusts

An individual can create a trust during his or her lifetime or in his or her will. Trusts created during one's lifetime are called *inter vivos* or *living trusts;* trusts created in a decedent's last will and testament are *testamentary trusts.* A testamentary trust does not come into being until the grantor dies. Many properly handled estate plans call for both testamentary and inter vivos trusts. This book will focus principally upon the use of the inter vivos trust as a vehicle for the increasing of wealth and income as well as the betterment of society.

A trust can be designed to accomplish any number of goals—to manage assets for minor or incompetent beneficiaries is just one function—but all trusts will be either revocable or irrevocable and will be testamentary or inter vivos. Understanding the basic nature of trusts and their operation calls for a special vocabulary. Before we go any further, let's consider a few of the terms with which we'll need to be familiar in order to fully understand trusts.

GRANTOR—That's you, if you set up a trust. The grantor is the creator of the trust and may also be called the *settlor* or *trustor.* Later in the book we will be discussing at some length how people benefited greatly by their creating a trust which helped them avoid taxes or increase their income. These people are grantors, and they may be sole grantors or co-grantors—if, for example, a spouse joined in the trust.

TRUSTEE—That may be you, too. When assets are transferred to a trust, those assets are no longer owned by the person who transferred them; their ownership now vests in the trust. The trustee is the person who is responsible for managing those assets subject to the directions provided by the trust document through which the trust was established.

The terms of the trust may be very restrictive, giving the trustee little or no latitude in how the trust is managed, or they may give the trustee considerable discretion. The trustee has the legal obligation to manage the trust prudently. Furthermore, if the trust has granted the trustee discretionary powers, the trustee must act impartially with respect to the beneficiaries.

Although you, as the grantor, could be the trustee (and, often, will be), there may be good reasons for appointing a corporate trustee either as a co-trustee or as the sole trustee. A corporate trustee might be a bank or a trust company.

BENEFICIARY—As indicated earlier, the beneficiary of the trust is the person who owns the beneficial interest in the trust. In simpler terms, this is the person or persons who will benefit from the operation of the trust by receiving income from the trust, a distribution of trust assets or both. In the trust arrangements we will be exploring, there will be two categories of beneficiaries: income beneficiaries and remainder beneficiaries (also called *remaindermen*). The grantor of the trust will often also be a beneficiary.

Charitable Remainder Trusts

The *charitable remainder trust* (CRT) is an irrevocable inter vivos trust and the principal trust vehicle we will be using to accomplish a large number of unexpected and highly desirable goals for the grantor. As in all trusts, there is a split in the ownership of the assets held in the trust.

Legal title is held by the trustee in his or her capacity as a trustee. (This is an important distinction since the grantor is often a trustee.) Beneficial interest is held by the beneficiaries. In the case of a charitable remainder trust, there are two categories of beneficiaries: income beneficiaries and remaindermen. The remainder beneficiary is a qualified charity or charities. The income beneficiary may be anyone designated by the grantor, but it is usually the grantor, himself, who is the income beneficiary.

REMAINDER BENEFICIARY—The remainder beneficiary of a charitable remainder trust is the charitable organization that, under the terms of the trust document, will receive the remainder of the trust assets when the income beneficiary's interest terminates.

INCOME BENEFICIARY—The income beneficiary of a charitable remainder trust is the person or persons who will receive an income from the assets held in the trust until the income beneficiary's interest terminates. According to charitable remainder trust rules, the income beneficiary can receive income for either a period of up to twenty years, or the life (or lives) of the income beneficiary or beneficiaries (a period that can be greater than twenty years).

Usually the grantor is an income beneficiary either by himself or herself—or with another person such as a spouse or child.

Trust Operation

The charitable remainder trust operates by providing an income to the income beneficiary or beneficiaries until the income interest terminates. At that time, the assets flow to the charity. Using the charitable remainder trust to provide income allows the grantor to avoid income taxes on the sale of property that has grown in value (thereby increasing his or her income, sometimes dramatically) and provides the grantor with a current charitable income tax deduction.

We will discuss the replacement for the heirs of the value of the gifted asset in considerable detail later. For now, it is important to realize that the value of the heirs' inheritance need not be reduced because of your use of this powerful wealth-generating tool.

Sometimes the easiest way to understand how something like a trust works is to use an example. Let's consider a hypothetical case, in which a person who is about to retire—let's call him Bob Smith—wants to increase his retirement income by selling some land and investing the proceeds. Let's further assume that he bought the land thirty years ago for $25,000 and, because of both residential and commercial development, the land is now valued at $2 million net of sales commissions. His federal income tax bracket is 39.6 percent, and he believes it is reasonable to expect a return on these invested assets of 8 percent.

Let's work out the numbers to see just what Bob would have as additional income after the sale of his property. First let's determine Bob's gain on the sale:

Property market value	$2,000,000
Cost basis	− 25,000
Taxable gain	$1,975,000

The value of the property had grown substantially since Bob had purchased it, but he hadn't realized that the gain was so large. A significant amount of the proceeds would be left to invest for income, but first we need to calculate the amount of taxes that would need to be paid.

Capital gain	$1,975,000
Capital gain tax rate	× 20%
Capital gain tax	$ 395,000
State income tax (7%)	+ 138,250
Total taxes on sale	$ 533,250

This may seem like an unusually high tax for Bob to pay, but it's the price he would have to pay to free up the capital in the land. We can determine the amount of capital that would be available to provide Bob's income by the following calculation:

Sale proceeds	$2,000,000
Taxes	− 533,250
Net to invest	$1,466,750

And Bob's investment income from the proceeds of the land sale can be calculated as follows:

Invested proceeds	$1,466,750
Rate of return	× 8%
Annual income	$ 117,340

Bob had hoped for a larger investment income, since he wanted to spend his retirement in places he had only dreamt about—places like Cairo and Beijing, Berlin and Johannesburg. Still, not many people realized such wonderful growth in their assets. But, it is still possible for him to avoid paying taxes on this gain. I am not talking about tax evasion. In fact, Bob can avoid taxes in ways both sanctioned and rewarded by the federal government.

Rather than selling the property, he could gift the property to a charitable remainder trust. Since the trust pays no income taxes, it could sell the property and have the entire $2 million available to produce income. Here is how the income results that would apply using the charitable remainder trust would change:

Property market value	$2,000,000
Cost basis	− 25,000
Capital gain	$1,975,000

At this point nothing has changed.

Capital gain	$1,975,000
Capital gain tax rate	× 00%
Total tax on gain	$ 00

Since there was no tax to be paid on the sale of the appreciated property, all of the proceeds would be available to produce an income—for Bob. The revised income calculation certainly looks more appealing:

Invested proceeds	$2,000,000
Rate of return	× 8%
Annual income	$ 160,000

The additional $42,660 each year in increased earnings amount to a 36 percent increase. Over the twenty years of Bob's remaining life expectancy, the increased income would amount to almost an additional million dollars. With this additional income, his dreams of travel look more feasible. This would be very pleasing news to Bob, but there is more to this. By making a charitable gift of his property, Bob is eligible for a tax deduction:

Value of property gifted	$2,000,000
Present value of income to Bob	− 1,301,760
Charitable income tax deduction	$ 698,240

Although the property gifted to the trust had a value of $2 million, the income that Bob would receive also has a value, and that value must be subtracted from the value of the property to determine the charitable income tax deduction. The actual value to Bob of this income tax deduction can be determined as follows:

Income tax deduction	$698,240
Bob's income tax bracket	× 39.6%
Value of the deduction in Bob's tax bracket:	$276,503

The value of the income tax deduction when added to the additional income Bob expected to realize over the next twenty years amounted to $1.2 million. By giving away the appreciated property—property that was going to be heavily taxed anyway—he was able to increase his income significantly.

This particular trust has two classes of beneficiaries: a current income beneficiary—Bob in this case—and a remainder beneficiary, which would be the charitable organization. In the above example, the trust allowed Bob the income to travel and gave him a big tax deduction as well.

This may sound too good to be true, but let's take a closer look at charitable gifts and how they developed, in order to better understand them.

Government's Protective Role

From the earliest times, the principal role of government has been the protection of its citizens. Initially, in the most rudimentary societies, people banded together to avoid being eaten by larger animals or being killed by other people. As more sophisticated societies evolved, the protection afforded by aggregation grew from simple defense against animals or bloodthirsty neighbors to include the defense against individual starvation or exposure to hostile elements.

Society became increasingly complex as its population grew. Occupations took on greater specialization; industrialization began; and modern monetary systems replaced bartering. In the United States, as immigration exploded, industrialization bloomed and family farms often became a distant, if charming, memory. Individuals and families who once provided for themselves became increasingly dependent on a young and unstable economy for the satisfaction of their most basic needs for food and shelter.

Churches, especially those serving immigrant and other populations with high levels of basic needs, often replaced the extended family as the first line of defense against hunger and other privations. Fraternal and charitable societies filled various niches, and government played an increasingly dominant role as the level of need escalated and the world was thrown into an abyss of economic depression.

BECAUSE OF THE ENORMOUS MECHANISM AND FUNDAMENTAL INEFFICIENCY OF MODERN GOVERNMENT, MORE MONEY IS REQUIRED— WHEN SUPPLIED BY GOVERNMENT—TO MAKE $1 AVAILABLE TO THE NEEDY. . . .

> While it was clear that the vast resources of the federal government were needed to meet basic needs on the grand scale presented by the depression of the 1930s, it was also clear that absolute reliance on government largesse meant that some of the needy would fall through the cracks. In addition, because of the enormous mechanism and fundamental inefficiency of modern government, more money is required—when supplied by government—to make $1 available to the needy than when made available through "provider-level" charities.

Government was quick to recognize that certain delivery of goods and services to the needy could best be effected through private charity, and the encouragement to philanthropy provided by tax deduction was written into tax law. So, the tax advantages which make the charitable remainder trust so attractive are grounded in society's need—not in a "tax loophole" created for the wealthy.

Income Tax Deduction for Charitable Gifts

Let's talk about the actual deduction provided by a contribution to a charitable remainder trust. To do that, it might be best to first consider the tax treatment given to an outright gift to a charity. If you made a gift of $1,000 to your church or to the American Cancer Society, you would be able to claim an immediate deduction of that $1,000. In other words, you could reduce your income for tax purposes in the year in which the gift was made by $1,000.

Determining the income tax deduction available for a gift made through a charitable remainder trust requires an additional step. You may remember that we alluded, briefly, to two beneficiaries—a current income beneficiary, which would be you, and a remainder beneficiary, which would be the charity. To calculate the income tax deduction, we need to determine the present value—the value today—of a gift of that remainder interest that may be made years in the future. Let's return to the numbers in Bob's situation.

If he gave away the property worth $2 million directly to a charity, he would be able to take a current deduction for the whole amount, subject, of course, to any limitation on the extent of the deduction based on his income. That's pretty simple. When we use a charitable remainder trust to structure our gift, however, we need to think of that $2 million as having a value comprised of two parts: the "current use" part and the "eventual ownership" part. In a charitable remainder trust, the eventual ownership part is given away.

The big job is calculating the value of that eventual ownership, i.e., the remainder that, at the end of the current use period, becomes a part of the charity's assets. Here's how it is done:

Current value of the property	−	Value of the income interest	=	Value of the remainder interest

The first task is to put a value on the income that you will receive from the trust. Once that is done, all you need to do is subtract that from the current value of the property to determine the value of the remainder interest—which you can deduct. Although there are two types of charitable remainder trust—the annuity trust and the unitrust—and the deductions are somewhat different, we will calculate the deduction based on a unitrust arrangement, in which the annual payment is determined by the payout percentage (established in the trust document) *applied to the current value of the trust.*

Since we assumed that Bob's annual income would be 8 percent, let's calculate the value of the income interest based on 8 percent. The IRS valuation tables for a single life at age sixty-five, calling for an 8 percent annual payment, tell us that the income interest is slightly more than 65 percent of the value of the property placed in the trust, leaving about 35 percent (since both interests must add up to 100 percent) as the value of what remains after deducting the value of the income interest. The actual numbers are .65088 for the income interest and .34912 for the remainder interest. Since we know the factors, we can now apply them to the actual numbers.

Current value of property	$2,000,000
Current income value factor	✕ .65088
Current income value	$1,301,760
Current value of property	$2,000,000
Current income value	− 1,301,760
Value of remainder interest	$ 698,240

Now that we know the present value of the remainder interest, we know that the income tax deduction is $698,240. The deduction would be different if a second type of charitable remainder trust were used— the annuity trust. Let's consider the annuity trust now.

The Unitrust and the Annuity Trust

The fundamental difference between the charitable remainder unitrust and the charitable remainder *annuity* trust is in how the annual income is determined. The annuity trust format is, by far, the simpler of the two, but it also allows for far less flexibility.

CHARITABLE REMAINDER ANNUITY TRUST—Using the annuity trust format, the annual income payout is unchangeable. Although the law requires that the percentage distributed each year not be less than 5 percent of the *initial trust assets,* the amount selected may be greater than that. That payment is made each year and will not vary as long as the trust contains sufficient assets to make the payment. So, if the grantor selected a charitable remainder annuity trust, the payments would remain level despite the fluctuating value of the trust corpus. For example, the trust cash flows might look like this:

8% CHARITABLE REMAINDER ANNUITY TRUST CASH FLOWS

INITIAL TRANSFER $2,000,000

YEAR	1	2	3	4	5
Return on assets	10%	9%	3%	10%	4%
Earnings	$200,000	$183,600	$61,908	$196,551	$80,082
End of Year assets	$2,040,000	$2,063,600	$1,965,508	$2,002,059	$1,922,141
Income payout	$160,000	$160,000	$160,000	$160,000	$160,000

CHARITABLE REMAINDER UNITRUST—Unlike the relatively simple charitable remainder annuity trust, the charitable remainder unitrust has three distinct format types.

- Type one (the standard payout option)
- Type two (the net income payment option)
- Type three (the net income with makeup option)

In a charitable remainder unitrust designed in a type-one format, the income beneficiary receives an income equal to the percentage of *current* trust assets. The percentage does not change, but since the trust assets probably will from year to year, the income also changes. Note the difference between the annuity trust, which we considered earlier, and the type-one unitrust: under the annuity trust, the income paid is the initial percentage chosen of the *initial trust assets;* under the type-one unitrust, the income paid is the initial percentage chosen of the *current trust assets.* Using the same percentage return on assets and the same initial percentage payout, the trust cash flows might look like this:

8% CHARITABLE REMAINDER UNITRUST TYPE ONE CASH FLOWS

INITIAL TRANSFER $2,000,000

YEAR	1	2	3	4	5
Return on assets	10%	9%	3%	10%	4%
Earnings	$200,000	$183,600	$61,812	$195,738	$79,861
End of year assets	$2,040,000	$2,060,400	$1,957,380	$1,996,528	$1,916,667
Income payout	$160,000	$163,200	$164,832	$156,590	$159,722

The important difference is obvious. In the case of the annuity trust, $160,000 was paid in income each year, despite the change in trust assets from year to year. In the type-one unitrust, the income payments increased as the value of the trust assets increased. (There is an obvious income downside, of course. If the trust assets decreased, the income would also decrease.) Note, also, that the income received by the income beneficiary *was not limited to the trust earnings*—year five trust earnings were only half of the income paid to the income beneficiary. To cover the topic more completely, let's consider the other two unitrust formats.

In the type-two unitrust, the trust distributes as income to the income beneficiary the *lesser* of the income percentage (8 percent in our illustration) and the income actually earned by the trust. Trust income is generally defined (subject to state law) to include dividends, interest, rents, royalties, and the discount elements of zero coupon bonds. It does not generally include capital gains.

If we assume that none of the income realized by the trust was capital gains, the trust cash flows of a type-two unitrust using the same percentage payout and return on assets might look like this:

8% CHARITABLE REMAINDER UNITRUST TYPE TWO CASH FLOWS

INITIAL TRANSFER $2,000,000

YEAR	1	2	3	4	5
Return on assets	10%	9%	3%	10%	4%
Earnings	$200,000	$183,600	$61,812	$206,040	$84,064
End of year assets	$2,040,000	$2,060,400	$2,060,400	$2,101,608	$2,101,608
Income payout	$160,000	$163,200	$61,812	$164,832	$84,064

In the type-three unitrust, the trust distributes as income to the income beneficiary the *lesser* of the income percentage (8 percent in our illustration) and the income actually earned by the trust, but *any income distribution less than 8 percent in a year will cause a deficit account to be created, to be paid to the income beneficiary at a later date when the trust income exceeds the income percentage.*

As we did before, let's look at the cash flows, this time of a type-three unitrust.

8% CHARITABLE REMAINDER UNITRUST TYPE THREE CASH FLOWS

INITIAL TRANSFER $2,000,000

YEAR	1	2	3	4	5
Return on assets	10%	9%	3%	10%	4%
Earnings	$200,000	$183,600	$61,812	$206,040	$82,416
End of year assets	$2,040,000	$2,060,400	$2,060,400	$2,060,400	$2,060,400
Income payout	$160,000	$163,200	$61,812	$206,040	$82,416

The amounts shown as trust income are for illustration purposes only, to show the operation of the trust and the income payments made under differing trust income assumptions. The year-to-year changes in trust income depend entirely upon the performance of the financial vehicle or vehicles in which the trust assets are invested and may be more or less than illustrated.

Just based on the assumptions used to illustrate the differing cash flows under the different types of charitable remainder trusts, we see the following results:

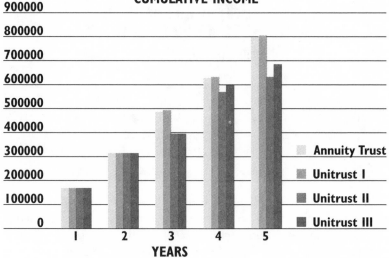

TYPE-TWO AND TYPE-THREE UNITRUSTS ALLOW THE GRANTOR TO *DEFER INCOME.*

Looking at the cumulative trust income charted graphically, it is natural to wonder why any grantor would want to fund a type-two or three unitrust. All things being equal, the annuity trust would usually provide the largest income when trust assets are earning less, on average, than the selected income percentage, and the type-one unitrust could use trust principal to make an income payment equal to the selected income percentage, while the type-two or three trusts are limited to making income payments *only* from trust earnings. The answer, of course, is that not all things are equal—especially the grantors' objectives. Among other planning advantages, type-two and type-three unitrusts allow the grantor to *defer income.*

This gives the grantor considerable planning flexibility; for example, the trust could be used to provide a retirement income, which could be especially useful for the person who is concerned about the taxation problem faced by our hapless examples in chapter 1. So, the selection of an annuity trust or a unitrust usually depends upon two factors: the need for income stability and the desire for the possibility of income growth—for example, to offset the erosion in buying power caused by inflation.

Tax Consequences of Selecting a Payout Rate and Trust Type

Since the value of the remainder interest—the amount that will eventually go to the charity—is significantly affected by the selected trust income rate, the income tax deduction for the gift to a charitable remainder trust will also depend upon the trust income rate selected. The higher the income rate selected, the lower the remainder interest and, consequently, the lower the immediate income tax deduction. For planning purposes, this means, of course, that maximizing the charitable income tax deduction requires establishing the lowest possible income rate—not a typical planning objective.

The extent of the current income tax deduction is also affected by the type of charitable remainder trust selected. Depending on payout rate and age of the annuitant, the annuity trust may yield a larger charitable contribution deduction[9] than a unitrust providing the same trust term and initial income.

Qualified Charitable Contributions

We need to understand, as we begin, that tax law is considered even by the experts to be difficult and ambiguous. One federal judge likened the difficulty of understanding certain provisions of the Internal Revenue Code to ". . . capturing a drop of mercury under your thumb."[10] Knowing that this subject is still being interpreted—and probably will be for hundreds of years—and may change at any moment, let's plow ahead with a discussion of income tax deductions.

In tax law, generally, when we talk of something as being "qualified," we mean that it qualifies for a current income tax deduction. Certainly, we may make a gift of property to any person or organization we choose; it's our asset, and, within limits, we may decide what to do with it. The issue, of course, is not what we are permitted to do with it; the issue is whether we may take an income tax deduction upon our making

---

[9] Stephan R. Leimberg et al. *The Tools and Techniques of Estate Planning* (Cincinnati, Ohio: National Underwriter Company, 1992).
[10] Weingarden v. Comm'r, 86 T.C. 669.

the gift for (a) its value, (b) some portion of its value, or (c) none of its value.

A gift from a parent to a child is a common and, often, tax-efficient method of transferring assets from one generation to another. Although the gift, depending upon its size relative to the number of donors (father or mother only versus father and mother jointly), may avoid gift—and, subsequently, estate—taxes, its value is not income tax deductible to the giver as a charitable gift. So, as much as we might view our children as a charity, current tax law doesn't provide a charitable deduction.

A gift to a charity will qualify for a current income tax deduction only if the charity is considered qualified. To be considered qualified, the charity must be a domestic organization and meet three conditions:

1. It must be operated exclusively for educational, charitable, religious, scientific, or literary purposes; the fostering of amateur sports competitions; or the prevention of cruelty to animals or children.

2. The organization's earnings may not benefit a private shareholder.

3. The organization must not have been disqualified for a tax exemption because of its lobbying or political activities.

In other words, the organization must really be organized with and operate for a charitable intent rather than a self-interested or political one. If an income tax deduction is important, you should make sure before choosing the charity that it is qualified. But does the charity need to be one of the high-profile variety, or are there choices? The answer is that there are choices, and the two principal choices are either a *public charity* or a *private foundation*. We will explore the non-tax benefits of each of the choices later; for now, let's examine what each choice means from an income tax perspective.

The general rule is that charitable contributions are deductible up to 50 percent of a taxpayer's *contribution* base. For most people, that contribution base is their adjusted gross income for tax purposes. Now, that's the general rule. However, since much of our interest involves the contribution of appreciated property and may involve a *private foundation*, the general rule undergoes considerable modification. Let's consider the difference between the tax treatment of property contributed to a public charity and the treatment of that same property contributed to a private foundation. Before we do, we should define what we mean by a private foundation. Essentially, a private foundation is an organization established to provide contributions to charities and that continues to be under the control of the donor or his or her designees.

The current tax law treats contributions to public charities more favorably than it treats similar contributions to private foundations. As an example, simple cash contributions that you might make to a public charity—the United Way, American Red Cross, etc.—are deductible, in the year made, up to 50 percent of your contribution base. (Remember, for most of us that's our adjusted gross income.) The same contribution made to a private foundation would allow you a current tax deduction up to only 30 percent of your contribution base. Since the deduction may be carried over to the following five years (making the gift deductible over a six-year period), in many cases, the difference may only be in the time value of money ($1 received today is generally more valuable than $1 received five years from today). Consider the following example of a donor in a 39.6 percent federal income tax bracket with a contribution base of $500,000 making a $900,000 cash gift:

TAX TREATMENT OF CASH GIFT COMPARISON

YEAR	PUBLIC CHARITY DEDUCTION	CASH FLOW	NVP AT 8%	PRIVATE FOUNDATION DEDUCTION	CASH FLOW	NPV AT 8%
1	$250,000	$99,000	$99,000	$150,000	$59,400	$59,400
2	250,000	99,000	91,664	150,000	59,400	54,998
3	250,000	99,000	84,873	150,000	59,400	50,924
4	150,000	59,400	47,152	150,000	59,400	47,152
5	0			150,000	59,400	43,659
6	0			150,000	59,400	40,428
Total	$900,000	$356,400	$322,689	$900,000	$356,400	$296,560

Since the donor making the charitable contribution to his private foundation was limited to a deduction of only 30 percent of his adjusted gross income, the entire gift was deducted over the full six-year period. The donor making the charitable contribution to the public charity, however, was able to exhaust the deduction over a four-year period. As a result of the greater earlier deductions, the net present value assuming an 8 percent discount rate was more than $26,000 greater for the donor to the public charity.

The charitable donor making gifts of cash to a public charity enjoys a more favorable tax treatment of the gift. But what about gifts of appreciated property, particularly gifts of long-term capital gain stock or mutual fund shares? Are they treated differently than gifts of cash? In a very meaningful sense, the answer is yes. The maximum deduction permitted for gifts of appreciated property is limited to 30 percent of the contribution base when gifted to a public charity, and only 20 percent of the contribution base when gifted to a private foundation. Let's consider the same comparison for appreciated property having the same value as the previous cash gift.

TAX TREATMENT OF APPRECIATED GIFT COMPARISON

YEAR	PUBLIC CHARITY DEDUCTION	CASH FLOW	NVP AT 8%	PRIVATE FOUNDATION DEDUCTION	CASH FLOW	NPV AT 8%
1	$150,000	$59,400	$59,400	$100,000	$39,600	$39,600
2	150,000	59,400	54,998	100,000	39,600	36,666
3	150,000	59,400	50,924	100,000	39,600	33,949
4	150,000	59,400	47,152	100,000	39,600	31,434
5	150,000	59,400	43,659	100,000	39,600	29,106
6	150,000	59,400	40,428	100,000	39,600	29,952
Total	$900,000	$356,400	$296,560	$600,000	$237,600	$197,707

Notice in the comparison that, given the same facts as in the previous cash gift, the full value of the appreciated gift can only be deducted when operating under the rules relating to gifts to public charities. Since deductibility of the gift to a private foundation is limited to 20 percent of the contribution base, the full value of the gift cannot be deducted within the maximum six-year limit. The result is that—with these client facts—only $600,000 of the $900,000 gift is deducted when contributed to the private foundation, and the difference in present value of the tax deduction is $98,853—almost 11 percent of the gift!

This analysis is not intended to cause you to avoid creating a private foundation; they can provide substantial benefits, which we will examine later. My intention is to demonstrate the need for competent, informed counsel before setting such a course.

Naming a Trustee: Use of a Special Independent Trustee
The trustee is the person or institution charged with carrying out the provisions of the trust and is named by the grantor—you. Not only do

you name the trustee, you may also replace the trustee for any reason, or for no reason. As the grantor, you have considerable latitude with respect to trustees; in fact, you may even designate yourself as the trustee. If you think you might want to be your own trustee, you will want to consider and discuss with your counsel the appropriateness of employing a special independent trustee to serve along with you. There are three principal circumstances that call for considering a special independent trustee:

1. If the trustee is expected to exercise any discretion with respect to the distribution of income

2. If the contributed assets are hard to value, such as close corporation stock that is not listed on an exchange

3. If the trust will be expected to sell appreciated property

The reason why an independent trustee should be involved in trusts in these three circumstances is simple; an independent trustee avoids the problem of an appearance of possible manipulation. Since an independent trustee is *not* the grantor or related or subordinate to the grantor, his or her judgment will not be affected by self-interest.

In a charitable remainder trust, the special independent trustee would be given discretion concerning

- The valuing of any hard-to-value assets, such as nonlisted stock, etc.

- The sprinkling of income among income beneficiaries

- The disposing of any contributed assets

Selecting the Investment Vehicle

Once the contribution of assets to the charitable remainder trust is completed, those assets need to be invested. Since the trustee is required to manage the assets of the trust for the benefit of both the *income beneficiary*—that may be you—and the *charitable remainderman,* the trustee's job in this regard may be a particularly difficult one. Generally, the primary objective of the charity that will ultimately receive the assets in the trust is conservation of those assets; the primary objective of the income beneficiaries is, typically, maximizing income from the assets. In those cases in which maximizing income calls for asset growth, there is a possible conflict with the objectives of the charity.

In general, the trustee is expected to invest the corpus of a charitable remainder trust in assets that are diversified, easily valued, marketable, and can be expected to produce a reasonable rate of return. While there are certain restrictions and guidelines provided in the applicable law, especially in the Uniform Prudent Investor Act, a trustee investing in assets meeting those criteria will generally be acting within the law.

The Charitable Remainder Trust—A Vehicle for Making Good Things Happen

Throughout most of the remainder of this book, we will be dealing with the use of the charitable remainder trust and considering it principally from the perspective of its benefits to you, the grantor of the trust. It is important to understand, however, that the charitable remainder trust benefits not only the grantor—by enabling him or her to avoid taxes and increase income—but also the charity or charities named as remaindermen, the grantor's heirs, and even the government.

As we discussed in an earlier chapter, the government benefits through the efficiency of the more *direct* allocation of necessary funds to charitable organizations that philanthropy provides. In other words, it is generally less expensive overall to support charities directly than through the operation of government.

Other Trusts that Play a Part

While the principal tool that we will be using to effect all of the benefits to the grantor and charities is the charitable remainder trust, there are other trust vehicles that often come into play, and we should spend a little time discussing them. The *charitable lead trust* is, in a sense, just the opposite of a charitable remainder trust.

In the lead trust, the charity receives the *current income* from the trust, and the trust assets are paid to a noncharitable remainderman at the end of the trust term—which may be for a term of years, e.g., twenty years or for the life of the grantor. The remainderman may be anyone; for example, the remainderman may be a child, a grandchild, or even the grantor (called a *reversionary interest*). The planning motivation for creating this kind of trust is often the immediate charitable deduction available to the grantor, equal to the present value of the annuity payable to the charity. (An interesting note: Although the grantor receives a charitable income tax deduction in the first year, in each subsequent year the income payable to the charity is taxable to the grantor.) Although the charitable lead trust is mentioned for the sake of completeness, it is used far less than its better-known cousin, the charitable remainder trust.

. . . HEIRS MAY SEE THEMSELVES AS BEING POORER BY VIRTUE OF THE GIFT . . .

Another trust used—extensively, in the case of charitable giving—is what is commonly referred to as an *asset replacement trust*. The function of this trust is to replace for the grantor's heirs the value of the gifted asset. While charitable giving may make wonderful sense to the donor from both a philanthropic and a tax-planning perspective, the potential heirs may see themselves as being poorer by virtue of the gift. This trust is designed to change that. We will talk more about this trust later in the book, but a brief description is called for here.

Generally, in an asset replacement trust, the grantor makes an annual noncharitable gift to an irrevocable living trust, in the names of the trust's eventual beneficiaries, equal to the annual premium for a life insurance policy. The trustee applies for life insurance on the life of the grantor in an amount that may represent the replacement value of the gifted asset and pays the premium from the grantor's noncharitable gift.[11] At the time when the gifted asset is usually paid to the charity, i.e., at the death of the grantor or grantors, the life insurance is paid to the heirs.

Another trust vehicle that is employed in special cases is the *special needs trust*. Its purpose is to provide for the special needs of an individual—often a child or grandchild of the grantor—who is disabled. The grantor establishes a trust instead of making an outright gift, because the outright gift may make the disabled individual ineligible for government benefits such as Supplemental Social Security or Medicaid. Since these government benefits may pay for enormously expensive treatments, their loss could create a substantial burden for the individual. Creating a trust designed to provide for needs that are not provided for by those government benefits could result in the enhancement of the disabled individual's life *without jeopardizing government benefits*. This is a special area of the law, and you should seek out an attorney who has experience in arranging special needs trusts to work in concert with your estate planner. This is not an area for the inexperienced.

---

[11] Both the sequence of the life insurance application/trust creation and the right of the eventual beneficiaries to withdraw the noncharitable gift are critical issues that bear on the estate tax and annual gift tax exclusion, respectively; competent counsel is absolutely essential to producing the proper result.

4 Uses of the Charitable Remainder Trust

Tax Incentives

A charitable trust has the tax status of a charity. As a result, much of what we do while using the trust enjoys important tax advantages similar to those we find with outright charitable gifts. Those advantages include:

- A current income tax deduction
- Capital gains tax avoidance
- Estate tax reduction

The Income Tax Deduction

The current income tax deduction received by the grantor of a charitable remainder trust is equal to the current value of the asset placed in the trust less the present value of the income that will be received by the current income beneficiary—usually the grantor—before the gift is received by the charity. If a grantor placed property valued at $200,000 into the charitable remainder trust and received an income that had a total present value of $80,000, the tax deduction would be $120,000—the difference between the two.

For reasons that we will look at shortly, many assets placed in charitable remainder trusts are appreciated assets, which means that the asset's value has grown—often dramatically—since it was purchased. An example of such an appreciated asset might be stocks in that start-up company that you may have purchased for $10,000, which are currently worth $200,000.

Provided the remainder beneficiary of the gift is a public charity (rather than a private foundation), the income tax deduction permitted for contributions of these appreciated assets is limited to the asset's current value up to no more than 30 percent of the donor's adjusted gross income. Simply stated, a donor who has an adjusted gross income of $100,000 may take a charitable deduction of up to $30,000 in that year for a gift of an appreciated asset. Fortunately, the donor may carry over any unused charitable deduction for up to five additional years. In the case of the $200,000 gift resulting in a $120,000 tax deduction, the donor with a consistent adjusted gross income of $100,000 would take a $30,000 income tax deduction in the year the asset was transferred to the trust and a $30,000 income tax deduction in each of the next three years.

An important calculation that we haven't yet discussed is the one used to determine the present value of the income to be received by the current income beneficiary. (Remember, that is deducted from the value of the asset to determine the total tax deduction.) In a general sense, the present value of that income is determined by two key factors: the amount of income to be received each year and the number of years the income will be paid.

For simplicity, let's assume that you, the reader, are the grantor of the charitable remainder trust and will be its current income beneficiary. You have placed an asset worth $1 million into the trust. Since you are the creator of the trust, it is up to you to decide at what interest rate the trust will pay you. Although the minimum rate is 5 percent, it may be— and often is—more. Let's say you chose a charitable remainder annuity trust and decided you wanted to receive 8 percent each year. As a result, each year you would receive $80,000—8 percent of the $1 million placed in the trust. So we have determined the value of the first key factor; it is $80,000.

The second key factor is how long the income will be paid. Let's assume you are sixty-five years old and that the income will be paid for the remainder of your life. At age sixty-five, you can be expected to live another twenty years. As a result, the present value of your income, considering both your age and the 8 percent return rate, is equal to about 65 percent of your gift (.65088). The tax deduction value of your gift is the difference, or about 35 percent of the value of the gifted asset (1 − .65088 = .34912). If you wanted only a 7 percent return, the tax deduction value of the gifted asset would increase to almost 39 percent; at 9 percent, the tax deduction has reduced to 31.6 percent (.31610).

So, for a gift of $1 million made to a charitable remainder trust by a sixty-five-year-old donor who will receive $80,000 each year for the remainder of his or her life, the grantor/donor will receive a current income tax deduction of $349,120, which may be taken over the year the gift is made and the five succeeding years. If the donor is in a 39.6 percent federal income tax bracket, he or she will have received a federal income tax savings of $138,251. In addition, there may be state income tax savings.

What if you want the current income to be paid during the life of two people and terminate only upon the death of the survivor—perhaps during your life and that of your spouse? Let's assume that both of you are sixty-five years old. According to government tables, the last survivor, of you and your spouse, can be expected to live for an additional twenty-five years. That would mean, of course, that the present value of your current income would be greater since it would be paid for a longer period. In fact, the present value would increase from the previous 65 percent (for your life alone) to 77.5 percent (.77544) for the lives of both you and your husband or wife. For that reason, the tax deduction value of your gift would reduce to about 22.5 percent of the gift, or about $224,560.

So, the extent of your total income tax deduction resulting from your transfer of assets into a charitable remainder trust depends upon the total income you can be expected to receive: the more you can expect to receive, the lower the tax deduction. The second major tax advantage of charitable giving using the charitable remainder trust has to do with recognizing capital gains.

Capital Gains Tax Avoidance

Although the term *capital gains* is fairly common, let's define it for our purposes as the amount by which the proceeds from the sale of a capital asset exceed its original price. In common parlance, capital gains is the profit resulting from the sale of something you own and use for personal purposes, pleasure, or investment. It is distinguished from *ordinary income,* which is the income you receive from your labor or from invested capital.

We mentioned earlier that many assets placed in charitable remainder trusts are appreciated assets, simply assets whose value has grown and on which the gains have not yet been recognized for tax purposes. In other words, a capital gain would have to be recognized upon their sale. One of the principal reasons for using appreciated assets for charitable purposes is to avoid the recognition of capital gains upon the asset's sale. Let's take a look at two examples of fairly common situations resulting in significant income tax problems.

The Mom-and-Pop Business

Many giant businesses had humble beginnings. Often they were started with a good idea and two or three people with enormous reservoirs of energy and commitment. Just as often, they were begun on a shoestring. The business that has grown because of that commitment and energy may be worth hundreds or even thousands of times the owner's investment. Additional investments made in the business for capital improvements are depreciated over varying periods and may provide no current cost basis. At some point, the original owners often choose to retire and use the proceeds from the sale of the business to provide an income during their retirement. Consider this fairly typical example.

Over a thirty-year period, Jim and Patricia Benner, working side by side, built a small advertising company into a major regional competitor in the Kansas City market. A business that began with one copywriter/artist and one media salesman—Pat and Jim, respectively—now had an art department, a staff of copywriters, account execs, a large client list, and a business value of more than $8 million. Over the years, Pat and Jim dreamed of selling the business, investing the proceeds, and retiring to the Virgin Islands. The Benners' attempt to sell the business began, fortunately, with a meeting with the company's accountant.

He explained that, because the business grew principally due to their creative genius rather than through the infusion of large amounts of capital, they had virtually no cost *basis* in the business. Since cost basis is the total of their investment less any depreciation, the entire sale price they received for the business would be considered capital gains. The accountant did a quick calculation and told them the bad news— about $2,160,000[12] would need to be paid in federal capital gains and state income taxes when the capital gains were recognized. At an 8 percent investment rate, that meant that their retirement income would be reduced by about $172,800 each year.

The Medical Practice

The practice of medicine combines the rewards that come with providing a life-giving and life-saving service to mankind with an opportunity to build a strong financial future for your family. Unfortunately, in those environments that permit the practitioner to practice medicine unfettered by an employee-employer relationship, the physician must provide for his or her own financial future.

---

[12] Amount shown is based on a 20 percent federal capital gains tax rate and an average state income tax rate of 7 percent.

Dan Stevens, M.D., completed his orthopedic residency when he was thirty years old. After spending two years as an associate in a group practice, he realized that he needed to start a solo practice. After thirty-three years as a solo practitioner, he knows that, for him, it was the right decision.

The first six months on his own had been rough. The business part of being a physician didn't come easily; referrals from general practitioners and other specialists came slowly at first. Eventually, however, his practice grew and even became prosperous. He purchased vacant land near a new subdivision and built a professional building that quickly filled with other specialists.

When Dan began making serious retirement plans, he looked to his professional building as the asset that would allow him to do the traveling he and his wife had wanted to do for years. His retirement plan would provide their basic income, and profit from the sale of the building would be the frosting on the cake. The building had a net value of about $2 million, and its sale would produce about $150,000 each year in additional income. Dan's attorney suggested a meeting with a financial advisor to coordinate the sale of his practice with the building sale and, generally, to provide the focal point for his financial plans.

The planner was thorough and competent. He pointed out that selling the building may not be the best idea and outlined the tax consequences—more than a half million dollars would immediately be siphoned off to pay capital gains taxes. Since selling the building was critical to his retirement traveling plans, Dan didn't know what to do. Certainly, $1.4 million was far better than nothing—and he knew that many people weren't so fortunate—but he just hated to lose so much of its value in taxes.

The Charitable Remainder Trust Answer

Both of these tax problems are ones we run up against each day. Many people would be surprised that charitable giving may be the answer. After all, from a financial point of view, isn't that like cutting off your finger because you have a hangnail? Let's take a look at how a charitable remainder trust would resolve the capital gains tax problem.

Remember, since a charitable remainder trust is a charitable trust, it is tax-exempt. That is the basis of the charitable trust's effectiveness in avoiding capital gains taxes. Here is how a charitable remainder trust solves the capital gains tax problems encountered by Jim and Pat Benner and Doctor Stevens.

| | JIM & PAT BENNER | | DR. DANIEL STEVENS | |
	OUTRIGHT BUSINESS SALE	CHARITABLE REMAINDER TRUST SALE	OUTRIGHT BUSINESS SALE	CHARITABLE REMAINDER TRUST SALE
Sale proceeds	$8,000,000	$8,000,000	$2,000,000	$2,000,000
— Cost basis	— 0	— 0	— 0	— 0
Capital gains	$8,000,000	$8,000,000	$2,000,000	$2,000,000
× Tax rate[13]	× 27%	× 0%	× 27%	× 0%
Tax payable	$2,160,000	$ 0	$ 540,000	$ 0
Sale proceeds	$8,000,000	$8,000,000	$2,000,000	$2,000,000
— Tax payable	— 2,160,000	— 0	— 540,000	— 0
Net to invest	$5,840,000	$8,000,000	$1,460,000	$2,000,000
Net to invest	$5,840,000	$8,000,000	$1,460,000	$2,000,000
× 8%	× 8%	× 8%	× 8%	× 8%
Annual income	$ 467,200	$ 640,000	$ 116,800	$ 160,000
Increased income		$ 172,800		$ 43,200
Total income increase*		$3,456,000		$ 864,000

* Based on a life expectancy at age 65 of 20 years.

The capital gains avoidance provided by a charitable remainder trust—regardless of the actual capital gains tax rate—is a perfect example of the marrying of society's good with private gain. In the Benners' case, it meant an additional $172,800 each year in income; for Doctor Stevens, it not only meant an additional $43,200 of annual income, it meant that a lifelong dream of travel would be fulfilled; for the charities to which the remainder would eventually go, it meant $10 million with which to feed children, give homes to the homeless, or find the means to combat disease.

It should be clear that the current income tax deduction and the avoidance of capital gains are significant benefits provided by a charitable trust. Let's look at the final tax benefit of a charitable trust: reducing your estate taxes.

---

[13] State and federal tax rates combined.

Estate Tax Reduction

Earlier, when we looked at the nature of wealth, we made the observation that much of what we think we own isn't really ours at all. In no situation does that seem to be more true than with estate taxes.

The federal estate tax is a tax on a person's right to transfer property he or she owns at death; it is imposed on—and its magnitude is based on—the taxable estate. The size of the tax may be enormous, depending upon the size of the taxable estate—up to 55 percent! That's right, the federal estate tax alone may take more than half of what you own—or think you own.

Ownership, of course, is the key ingredient of assets that form a part of anyone's estate. Except for specific exceptions by virtue of which assets may be deemed to be owned by you, your estate is not taxed on property that you don't own. Just as ownership is the sine qua non of estate taxes, it is also the key to their reduction. An important technique for reducing your estate taxes is to give away your assets. Unfortunately, significant gifts made outright to your ultimate heirs create other problems for you. Two problems in noncharitable gift giving concern most donors:

- Once you give property away to your heirs, you also give away the income that property can produce.

- Noncharitable gifts incur a gift tax when they exceed a relatively modest value.

The answer may lie in the use of a charitable remainder trust. By giving all of your assets in excess of $1 million per individual to a charitable remainder trust you can effectively reduce your estate taxes to zero—without incurring any gift taxes. (The $1 million per individual is the amount that may be transferred tax free at death to anyone once the full effect of the Taxpayer Relief Act of 1997 is realized, in 2006.)

The charitable gift will result in a tax deduction and, in the case of the gift of appreciated assets, the avoidance of capital gains taxes. The avoidance of capital gains taxes will result in a larger amount of money to invest than if the asset had been sold (and taxes paid on the gain), thereby increasing your income—often, substantially. Since many—perhaps most—potential donors are reluctant to give away assets that would have been passed to their heirs, they often arrange to replace the value of the asset given away. This is done by taking the value of the tax deduction and a part of the increased income and gifting it into an irrevocable trust; the trustee, then, uses the gifted money to purchase life insurance to replace the value of the property that was gifted to the charitable remainder trust. The result is that our client has more income, the heirs have a larger inheritance, and a charity—maybe your private charitable foundation—has the funds to continue its charitable work.

We recognize, of course, that it may be inappropriate to transfer all of one's assets into a charitable remainder trust. That approach has been taken only to show how all estate taxes may be avoided, in order to demonstrate the principle. As with all of the tools and techniques we have discussed and will discuss in the upcoming pages, it is vitally important that you use competent counsel *before* employing any of these approaches. Doing so can save you a fortune—literally.

These are the principal tax reasons for using a charitable remainder trust in your estate planning. There are other—more human, I like to think—reasons for doing so. Let's shift our attention, now, to these reasons.

Financial Planning Incentives

One of the larger challenges in writing a book dealing with tax planning from the heart is the need—for the sake of simplicity—to deal with each benefit separately, while acknowledging that the benefits, themselves, are almost inextricably entwined. The financial planning motivation for the employment of a particular technique to enhance income often relies on tax incentives; yet, to attempt to deal with the issue completely by moving down each of the tortuous pathways simultaneously would result in a book enjoyed—and I use that term in its broadest sense—only by my CPA friends. With that disclaimer firmly in place, let's proceed to the financial planning incentives for using charitable remainder trusts in your planning.

Keeping More of What You Have

It is hard to conceive of giving an asset away and simultaneously having more of it; in fact, it sounds more like a tale from the brothers Grimm than sound advice on tax planning. This phenomenon occurs, in part, because of the tax on appreciated assets, which is avoided through the use of a charitable remainder trust. Using a charitable remainder trust permits you to completely avoid the payment of capital gains taxes and enjoy additional tax benefits—which translate into cash—arising from the income tax deduction. The result is a reduced asset outflow to pay taxes—ordinary income taxes and capital gains taxes—and a substantial increase in the net amount available to invest.

Increasing Spendable Income

An increase in your spendable income arises directly from the increase in the net amount to invest caused by the avoidance of capital gains and the sizable income tax deduction.

The outright sale of an appreciated asset may reduce the net sale proceeds by as much as 27 percent, based on the current federal capital gains tax rate and state income taxes on the gain. By avoiding that capital gains tax through the use of the charitable remainder trust, your income—assuming the same rate—is increased by up to 27 percent— or more if state taxes are greater than 7 percent. Furthermore, the income tax on much of the early income derived from the assets in the charitable remainder trust may be avoided because of the income tax deduction you receive for putting the assets in the trust.

Transferring More Wealth to Children and Grandchildren

By employing a charitable remainder trust, the transfer of substantial additional wealth to heirs is accomplished through a process that is, simply, more tax efficient than a lifetime sale of an asset and a subsequent bequest. By way of example, let me offer a comparison between the sale of a piece of appreciated property and its transfer to a charitable remainder trust.

The first erosion of the asset upon sale is caused by the payment of taxes on the gain—federal capital gains taxes and state income taxes; the second erosion of the remaining asset is caused by estate taxes. Both of these taxes are avoided in the tax-wise approach using the charitable remainder trust. Using the charitable remainder trust, our client creates an additional trust, called an irrevocable life insurance trust, which purchases life insurance on the client's life equal to the value of the gifted asset—in this case, $1 million—paid for by the tax savings arising out of the gift and the increased income created by avoiding the capital gains taxes. Let's look at the comparison.

	SALE OF THE ASSET	CHARITABLE REMAINDER TRUST
Sale proceeds	$1,000,000	$1,000,000
— Cost basis	— 0	— 0
Capital gains	$1,000,000	$1,000,000
× Tax rate (state & federal)	× 27%	× 0%
Capital gains tax	$ 270,000	$ 0
Sale proceeds	$1,000,000	$1,000,000
— Capital gains tax	— 270,000	— 0
Net to invest	$ 730,000	$1,000,000
Asset value at death	$ 730,000	$1,000,000
× Estate tax rate*	× 55%	× 0%
Estate tax payable*	$ 401,500	$ 0
Asset value at death	$ 730,000	$1,000,000
— Estate tax payable	— 401,500	— 0
Asset passed to heirs	$ 328,500	$1,000,000

* Based on a total taxable estate of $3,000,000 or more.

The benefit to the heirs is obvious: They receive an inheritance of more than three times what they would have received if the asset had been sold outright.

Protecting Assets From Creditors

Although protection of assets from the claims of creditors would not usually seem to be a compelling reason to establish and fund a charitable remainder, it is, nonetheless, a result of transferring assets into an irrevocable trust. Since the assets are no longer owned by the grantor, they are no longer subject to the claims of his or her creditors.

Endowing Your Favorite Charities

Can anyone stroll down Duke of Gloucester street in Colonial Williamsburg or consider the libraries funded by Andrew Carnegie and not be struck by the power of wealth to perform miracles? You and I may not have the great wealth of a Rockefeller or a Carnegie, but, through the power of a charitable remainder trust, we can invest our social capital to further the work of those charities that are important to us, while improving our own financial condition.

A charitable remainder trust allows us to change the *involuntary philanthropy* represented by our taxes into *voluntary philanthropy,* which enables us to control how our tax dollars are spent. It permits us to redirect our tax dollars to local social, medical, cultural, and religious organizations that we may already support. If you would prefer to see your social capital funding the local symphony or hospital instead of going to Washington to support the current administration's agenda, this may be your opportunity.

Who Is Most Likely To Benefit?

The people who can benefit from charitable tax planning—and from a charitable remainder trust, specifically—come from all walks of life and may have vastly different objectives. Interestingly, most clients had not even considered charitable tax planning when they first came to us. In many cases, they were simply interested in improving their financial situation, and we were contacted to help them do that. We are going to look at a number of people—actually, most of them are composites drawn from financial and estate planning practices—in the next few chapters who benefited from tax planning from the heart. Let's take a brief look at their situations.

The Brewers, a Midwestern farm couple in their late sixties, wanted to sell a part of their farm and supplement their retirement income with the earnings it could provide. They found their small cost basis resulted in high capital gains taxes, and the sales proceeds left after taxes would be insufficient to provide the needed income.

The Lincolns, a retired couple in their early seventies who found the income from their stocks to be too low to support the lifestyle they had enjoyed while they were working, wanted primarily to increase their investment income and diversify their assets by restructuring their investment portfolio. They found, unfortunately, that selling their stock would result in a loss of more than $240,000 due to capital gains and income taxes, and would reduce their income instead of increase it.

The Kirtlands, a couple who owned and operated a metal fabricating business, received an offer to sell the business. Since they were approaching retirement age, the offer couldn't have been more timely—and it was a reasonable offer. They were prepared to accept the offer and retire, when they realized that capital gains taxes would leave insufficient capital to provide a livable income; reluctantly, they had to decline.

Max Lyle, an entrepreneur who built a business from scratch to one worth more than $5 million, wants to sell the business and produce a high level of after-tax income. His problem—a tax bill of almost $1.4 million.

The Casses, a successful consulting engineer and his wife, nearing retirement, have just learned that the funds he accumulated in his pension plan will be subject to a combination of income and estate taxes at their death amounting to almost 70 percent.

The Pearsons, owners and managers of a manufacturing business worth about $4 million, have been supporters of various local charities. They want to leave a substantial gift to those charities instead of paying taxes, while leaving a large inheritance to their children. Unfortunately, their business has very little cost basis.

Joan Lerner is a senior executive in her mid-forties who has accumulated substantial stock options. Her business is thriving—resulting in significant growth in the value of her company's stock that she holds, but she is concerned that all of her retirement "eggs" are in one basket. She wants to diversify. Unfortunately, her modest cost basis will result in large capital gains on which to pay taxes. Her use of a charitable remainder trust will allow her to diversify and increase her lifetime income about 55 percent.

Mrs. Grant is a widow, age seventy, who has about half of her assets inside a qualified plan begun by her husband. Her retirement assets will incur a 50 percent estate tax and 39.6 percent income tax. She has realized that, while a pension plan may be a great way to accumulate assets, it is a terrible way to distribute them.

The Wilburs are in their late forties. He has a successful private practice as a family practice physician and has been setting aside money in his pension plan. He is concerned, however, that this will be insufficient to provide an adequate retirement income. In addition, the Wilburs have just made their last mortgage payment and now have an additional $30,000 to invest each year. They found a charitable trust was a marvelous way to maximize their assets and produce a flexible source of additional retirement income.

Benny Hernandez, a professional athlete from a humble environment, had seen other great athletes retire in poverty and was determined it wouldn't happen to him. He gave back to his community while enjoying, as a result, both increased income and a tax shelter.

In the next few chapters we will get to know each of these people much better and begin to understand how the powerful charitable remainder trust enabled them to meet their financial objectives—sometimes in unexpected ways.

5 Increasing Retirement Income

For many people, retirement represents an all-important return to a sort of sophisticated childhood, in which our days are spent playing, free of financial cares. For that reason, most people, when making financial decisions about major purchases or cash outlays, think about its effect upon their retirement and their retirement income. It is the most frequent reason that is given for saving and investing.

Not all retirement plans are provided through pensions or profit-sharing arrangements; many are a good bit less formal, even if no less important. We are going to visit with two couples in the next few pages, the Brewers and the Lincolns, who were concerned about their level of retirement income but who found that the remedy for their problem created an even larger problem—severe taxes. These couples came from completely different backgrounds; the Brewers were successful Midwestern dairy farmers, and not yet retired, while the Lincolns had retired seven years earlier after a career in industry.

The Brewers

Forty years ago, the Brewers married and began operating a modest dairy farm. As a result of a farmland inheritance and, over the years, their shrewd acquisition of property surrounding their farm, they came to own one of the largest farms in a community of large dairy farms. Because of their effort and skilled management, the dairy farm became a resounding success. But, forty years is a long time, and the continuing demands of a dairy farm have caused Claude and Nancy to grow weary. Now, at age sixty-seven, they would like to retire from farming altogether and spend more of their time with their grandchildren and working with their church.

Over the last several years, the Brewers have taken small steps towards retiring by selling off small parcels of the land and a few of their cows. Most of the remaining land has been leased to their neighbors to use as pastures for their animals. These steps, however, haven't produced sufficient income to enable Claude and Nancy to retire, nor have they freed up the time that they would like to spend doing other things.

The Brewers' five children have produced seven grandchildren, and none of the offspring are interested in farming. Although the family consensus is to keep the house and some of the adjoining farmland in the family, each of the children has carved out a career of his or her own in a neighboring city—culturally, far from the farm. Furthermore, each of the grandchildren has already begun on a career path, equally far from the routine of a dairy farm. It is clear to Claude and Nancy that the farm will eventually be sold, either during their life or that of their children.

The Brewers' Challenge

About ten years ago, the Brewers built a new milking barn with the latest in milking parlor technology, and it has added significantly to the farm's profitability. In large part because of this milking barn, the farm is considered one of the most advanced in the region and, according to the records of the cooperative, regularly outproduces its neighbors. The barn and milking parlor have been appraised at $300,000.

The Brewers' current income is derived from their milking operation, interest on a few certificates of deposit, Social Security, and the rent they receive from their leased pastureland. Right now, it is enough for their needs; in fact, they are fairly comfortable. Their concern is that their income would no longer be sufficient if they fully retired from the dairy operation. They considered selling the milking barn to an adjacent neighbor who offered the full $300,000 it was worth. Unfortunately, since they had almost no remaining cost basis in the barn, the entire $300,000 would be considered capital gains income, subject to tax. When they were told that $81,000 would be needed to pay the federal capital gains taxes and state income tax on the sale, they realized that the resulting $17,520 of annual supplemental income they could expect at 8 percent interest would not be enough to allow them to retire. As a result, they turned down the offer and continued the farming operation, disappointed but resigned.

Their dilemma was an obvious one. How could they afford to retire when taxes would take so much of the sale proceeds?

The Church's Need for Income Presents an Opportunity

The Brewers' local church, in an effort to encourage increased contributions and to provide a forum for tax and retirement ideas, sponsored a seminar on financial planning. As Nancy and Claude sat in the audience, it was almost as though the speaker, a financial planning expert, was talking directly to them. He talked about a way to sell property that had grown considerably in value, without having to pay taxes on the gain, while benefiting the church that was so much a part of their life. More than a little interested, at the break the Brewers arranged a private meeting with the speaker for the following week.

During the seminar, the financial adviser had discussed how people in situations similar to the Brewers' had used a charitable remainder trust to enhance their personal financial situation. The speaker talked about getting a tax break on the sale *and* keeping the income from the asset for as long as they lived. Although the Brewers supported the church regularly and had made provision for a substantial gift at their death, they had never before considered using a charitable trust.

When the adviser met with the Brewers, he explained again how they could use a charitable remainder trust to give them a supplemental lifetime income, avoid the federal capital gains and state income tax that would have consumed $81,000 of the barn's sale proceeds, and provide a gift to their church. Over a period of two additional meetings, and at the conclusion of a lengthy fact-finding interview, the Brewers established three objectives with respect to this piece of property. Those objectives were to

1. Supplement their retirement income for the rest of their life

2. Provide an inheritance to their children of $150,000

3. Make a significant gift to their church

Planning for the Brewers

The financial adviser acted as the focal point for a planning team, which included the Brewers' attorney and accountant. Acting together, the team developed a four-point plan designed to accomplish the Brewers' objectives. The plan was as follows:

1. The Brewers were to establish a charitable remainder trust and would name themselves as primary trustees. Into this trust, the Brewers would contribute their milking barn. An independent trustee, appointed by the Brewers, would sell the barn on behalf of the trust. The Brewers would, then, invest the proceeds from the barn's

sale. Since the trust was tax-exempt, the $81,000 of capital gains and state income tax that, formerly, ate a large hole in the sale proceeds would no longer be payable.

2. As a direct result of their contribution of the barn, the Brewers would receive an income tax deduction of approximately $97,000. In addition, since they are income beneficiaries of the trust, they would receive a yearly income of about $24,000 for as long as either of them continued to live—an annual increase of more than $6,700 compared to an outright sale of the barn.

3. Since the Brewers didn't want their contribution to decrease the size of their children's inheritance, they would create another trust, called a "wealth replacement trust," into which they would contribute $5,200 each year for ten years from their tax savings and increased income. The trustee would purchase a life insurance policy of $150,000, payable ultimately to the children, which would more than replace the after-tax value of the gifted property. The $150,000 would be free of either income tax or estate tax.

4. When the second of the two of them died, the $300,000 in the charitable remainder trust would pass to the church.

The financial planning team provided the Brewers with a financial analysis of the plan that looked at the comparative results in terms of (a) invested assets, (b) cash flow, and (c) estate taxes. In addition, they compared the resulting benefits to the children, the church, and the Brewers themselves. Following are the highlights of the financial analysis.

INVESTED ASSET ANALYSIS

	OUTRIGHT SALE	THE CRT PLAN
Value of the milking barn	$300,000	$ 300,000
less, remaining adjusted cost basis	− 0	− 0
Capital gain realized on the barn's sale	300,000	300,000
times, federal capital gains and state tax rate	× 27%	× 0%
Taxes paid on the barn's sale	81,000	0
Sale proceeds	$300,000	$ 300,000
less, taxes to be paid on the sale	− 81,000	− 0
Assets available to be invested	$219,000	$ 300,000

CASH FLOW ANALYSIS

	OUTRIGHT SALE	THE CRT PLAN
Annual gross income from invested asset (8%)	$ 17,520	$ 24,000
Annual net income after 31% tax	12,089	16,560
times, life expectancy	× 20	× 20
Lifetime net income	$241,780	$331,200
Charitable income tax deduction	$ 0	$ 97,000
times, the Brewers' income tax bracket	× 31%	× 31%
The Brewers' income tax savings	0	$ 30,070
Annual wealth replacement life insurance cost	0	5,200
times, number of years premium payable	× 0	× 10
Total life insurance cost	0	52,000
Brewers' lifetime net income	$241,780	$331,200
plus, income tax savings	0	30,070
less, total life insurance cost		52,000
Lifetime spendable income	$241,780	$309,270

ESTATE TAX ANALYSIS

	OUTRIGHT SALE	THE CRT PLAN
Barn's net sale proceeds in Brewers' estate	$219,000	$ 0
times, the Brewers' estate tax rate	× 55%	× 55%
Estate taxes payable	120,450	0
Net sales proceeds in Brewers' estate	$219,000	$ 0
less, estate taxes	− 120,450	− 0
Estate asset passed to the heirs	$ 98,550	$ 0
plus, life insurance passed to the heirs	+ 0	+150,000
Total passed to heirs	$ 98,550	$150,000

SUMMARY OF BENEFITS

AFFECTED PARTY	OUTRIGHT SALE	THE CRT PLAN	PERCENTAGE DIFFERENCE
Lifetime spendable income to the Brewers	$241,780	$309,270	+ 28%
Benefit to the children and grandchildren	$ 98,550	$150,000	+ 52%
Charitable gift to the church	$ 0	$300,000	!!!

The benefits to the Brewers, their children, and their church were obvious. In every case, the charitable remainder trust worked to produce more. The Brewers' lifetime spendable income was increased by 28 percent. The asset passed to the children at the Brewers' death grew from $98,550 to $150,000, an increase of 52 percent. (There were, of course, other assets passed to them.) Finally, the church that meant so much to them received $300,000 through the CRT plan instead of nothing. Everybody won.

For the Brewers, the power of the charitable remainder trust meant increased income, and it meant that, for the first time, they could really retire. After forty years, they were ready.

The Lincolns

The Lincolns retired seven years ago; Jim Lincoln, now age seventy-two, had been an executive with a public company, and his compensation had included a fairly generous stock option plan. Over his working years, he had exercised a number of options and had invested a total of $100,000 in company stock. The stock has continued to grow in value and is currently worth $1 million. Jim and his wife, Betty, are delighted with the stock's total return. Unfortunately, the stock's dividend yield— the part of that total return that provides current income—has never exceeded 3 percent. Although they are living comfortably, they are concerned that future inflation will change all that, and the low dividend yield will be insufficient to enable them to maintain their lifestyle.

Jim would like to sell some or all of the stock and invest the proceeds in a portfolio that will produce more income and provide greater diversification. However, the capital gains tax consequences have made that kind of an investment adjustment too costly. Jim estimated that only $757,000 of the $1 million would remain after taxes for investment if he sold all of the company stock and paid the income taxes. It just didn't seem sensible to Jim or Betty to take that action and pay almost a quarter million dollars to the IRS for the privilege. As a result of that quandary, they have not made any portfolio changes—even though they know they should.

The problem that the Lincolns have is a fairly common one. The numbers, of course, may be different but the dilemma is not unusual. It involves a Hobson's choice: If you want to sell the stock to buy higher-yield investments, you will probably have to pay federal capital gains and state income tax because the stock may have appreciated; however, if you hold onto the stock you will avoid the taxes, but you will have to live with a low-yield investment. Neither choice is satisfying.

The Lincolns' Objectives

Realizing that a misstep could be very costly, Jim and Betty consulted a financial adviser and described their situation to her. She scheduled a number of meetings with Jim and Betty and, after a long fact-finding session, presented to them a list of their objectives for their review. Those objectives were to

1. Increase their retirement income without incurring taxes

2. Reduce their current income tax

3. Diversify their assets for greater safety

4. Leave an inheritance to their children

5. Minimize their estate taxes

After reviewing the list of objectives, both Jim and Betty acknowledged that these were, indeed, what they wanted to do.

Both of the Lincolns had mentioned their charitable work, and the adviser asked them what kind of charitable work they did. Eagerly, Betty told the adviser of their work with the local sheltered workshop (a shop that employs only the handicapped). It was obvious that the workshop represented a serious emotional and physical commitment for both Jim and Betty. It was only much later that the adviser came to realize that the sheltered workshop had meant the difference between a life with meaning and one without meaning for someone very close to Betty. Her brother had been severely impaired and a long-time member of the workshop until his death. They had made generous provision for the workshop in both of their wills. The adviser asked if they would be interested in making a big financial difference for the sheltered workshop while solving their personal financial dilemma. Jim acknowledged that would be an ideal arrangement but expressed some skepticism it could be arranged.

The adviser explained social capital, the part of our wealth we can't keep. It is so named because it is the wealth used to benefit society, for social purposes. An example of that social capital is the tax the Lincolns would have to pay upon selling their appreciated stock. Although the payment of taxes is one way of transferring this social capital to others, it is not the only way. In fact, it may not be the best way for either the taxpayers or the recipients.

The Lincolns could make a dramatic gift to the workshop by contributing their stock to a charitable remainder trust. For that contribution they would receive an income tax deduction. The trust would then sell their stock and reinvest the proceeds to increase the portfolio's yield, which would increase Jim and Betty's income.

When the trust sold the low-yield stock, it would pay no taxes on the gain, since the trust is tax-exempt. So, the income the Lincolns could expect would be substantially higher than if they sold their stock themselves, because all of the proceeds could be used to provide income rather than pay taxes.

The Lincolns were concerned that they would be giving away their children's inheritance, but the tax benefits and increased income would allow the Lincolns to purchase life insurance to replace the value of the stock that was being donated. In fact, the inheritance left to their children would be far greater than they would receive otherwise. Their income would increase, their children's inheritance would be larger, and the sheltered workshop would receive a substantial gift—all by using a charitable trust.

It didn't take Jim and Betty long to acknowledge that the adviser had gotten their attention. They quickly scheduled a meeting with their accountant, their lawyer, the director of development at the sheltered workshop and, of course, their adviser. At the meeting the adviser outlined the proposed financial plan parameters, and the Lincolns asked the team to draw up a plan that would accomplish the objectives the adviser had verified with them.

The four-part plan looked like this:

1. The Lincolns would establish a charitable remainder trust and name themselves trustees in order to retain control of the trust's operation. To the trust they would give $600,000 of their stock, which would result in an income tax deduction of $180,000. In their income tax bracket, this deduction would save them $55,800 in federal income taxes.

2. The trust would then sell the $600,000 of appreciated stock and reinvest the proceeds in a highly diversified investment portfolio with an income orientation. Since no capital gains tax would be paid, the entire $600,000 of proceeds would be available to produce investment income. At an 8 percent annual distribution from the trust, the Lincoln's income derived from this investment would be $48,000, rather than the $18,000 it would have yielded if held.

3. The Lincolns would then create an additional trust called a "wealth replacement trust," designed to replace, for the children, the value of the gifted property. Into this trust, they would make annual gifts of $10,000 for ten years, which would be used to purchase $275,000 of life insurance owned by the trust and payable to the children.

4. When Jim and Betty died, the children would receive the $275,000 from the life insurance tax free, and the sheltered workshop would receive $600,000 with which to carry on their work with the handicapped.

The financial planning team, with Jim and Betty's approval, proposed the plan to the Lincoln's children at the same time it was presented to Jim and Betty. Because the children's inheritance would be affected, it was appropriate to include them in the decision-making process.

Let's take a closer look at what the advisers proposed, beginning by outlining the concerns that caused Jim and Betty to consider making changes in their investment portfolio, specifically, the desire to increase their retirement income to keep pace with inflation and to diversify their assets to avoid having to rely on the financial results of a single company for their income.

INVESTMENT ASSET ANALYSIS

	MAKE NO CHANGES	SELL THE STOCK OUTRIGHT	SELL THE STOCK USING A CRT
Value of the stock	$600,000	$600,000	$600,000
less, the Lincolns' cost basis	NA	− 100,000	− 100,000
Capital gains realized on the stock sale	NA	500,000	500,000
times, the federal and state tax rate	NA	× 27%	× 0%
Taxes paid on the stock sale	NA	135,000	0
Proceeds	$600,000	$600,000	$600,000
less, taxes to be paid on the stock sale	NA	− 135,000	0
Assets available for investment	$600,000	$465,000	$600,000

To fully appreciate the value of the proposed plan, it is important to focus attention on the portion of the investment portfolio that would be affected, specifically $600,000 of the appreciated stock. There are three basic choices: do nothing, sell the stock outright, or sell the stock using a charitable remainder trust. Those alternatives are shown on the investment asset analysis.

The cash flow analysis is designed to demonstrate the different income flows that result from the three options. The "do nothing" option means that, if the historic dividend yield continued, the income for Jim and Betty from this particular $600,000 of appreciated stock was probably not going to be much more than $18,000 each year. After taxes, it would provide a little more than $12,000 each year.

CASH FLOW ANALYSIS

	MAKE NO CHANGES	SELL THE STOCK OUTRIGHT	SELL THE STOCK USING A CRT
Annual gross income from investment*	$ 18,000	$ 37,200	$ 48,000
Annual net income after 31% tax	12,420	25,668	33,120
times, the Lincolns' life expectancy	✕ 16	✕ 16	✕ 16
Lifetime net income	$198,720	$410,688	$529,920
Charitable income tax deduction	$ 0	$ 0	$180,000
times, the Lincolns' tax bracket	✕ 31%	✕ 31%	✕ 31%
The Lincolns' income tax savings	$ 0	$ 0	$ 55,800
Annual life insurance premium	0	0	$ 10,000
times, number of years payable#	✕ 0	✕ 0	✕ 10
Total life insurance cost	0	0	100,000
Lincolns' lifetime net income	$198,720	$410,688	$529,920
plus, income tax savings	+ 0	+ 0	+ 55,800
less, total life insurance cost	— 0	— 0	— 100,000
Lifetime spendable income	$198,720	$410,688	$485,720

* Based on a 3 percent dividend yield on currently held securities and 8 percent on a restructured portfolio.

\# Based on the current dividend scale which is not guaranteed

Selling the stock outright would more than double the Lincolns' annual income. However, using the charitable remainder trust method would result in more than $11,000 of additional gross income (almost $8,000 of net income), compared to selling the stock outright. Although the life insurance to replace the value of the gifted stock for the heirs would result in some additional expense, when that was deducted from the lifetime income and the value of the tax deduction was added in, the result was an approximately 18 percent increase in lifetime spendable income over the result if the stock had been sold outright.

Of course, none of the income amounts shown are guaranteed. They're based on historical yields (in the case of the current stock portfolio) and an 8 percent yield assumption in the case of the restructured portfolios both outside and inside the trust.

Clearly, the selling of the stock inside the charitable remainder trust is the most advantageous route for Jim and Betty, yet it might seem to some observers that the trust could only reduce the value of the children's inheritance. After the reduction of the tax impact of both the income and estate taxes, however, none of the inheritance would be lost. In fact, the inheritance would be somewhat larger.

ESTATE ANALYSIS

	MAKE NO CHANGES	SELL THE STOCK OUTRIGHT	SELL THE STOCK USING A CRT
Value of the asset in the taxable estate	$600,000	$465,000	$ 0
times, the estate tax rate	$\times$ 55%	$\times$ 55%	$\times$ 55%
Estate tax payable on the asset	$330,000	$255,750	$ 0
Value of the asset in the taxable estate	$600,000	$465,000	$ 0
less, the estate tax payable	− 330,000	− 255,750	— 0
Value of the asset to the children	$270,000	$209,250	$ 0
plus, life insurance to the children	+ 0	+ 0	+ 275,000
Net benefit to the children	$270,000	$209,250	$275,000

If you look at the estate analysis, at the last number in the "Make No Changes" column you will see that the estate taxes would take $330,000 of the $600,000 asset when the second of Jim and Betty dies, leaving $270,000 for the children. If the stock had been sold outright to produce more income, the inheritance to the children would have been reduced even further, to $209,250, because of the federal capital gains and state income taxes that would have eroded the investment.

Finally, if you look at the last column—the one headed "Sell the Stock Using a CRT"—you will note that, although none of the gifted stock remained in the estate, the wealth replacement trust would pay the children $275,000, only $5,000 more than they would have received if the stock had never been sold but almost one-third more than if the stock had been sold outright and reinvested. In no case, would the children's interest be compromised. In fact, replacing the variable value of the stock with the certain value of the life insurance proceeds means that the inheritance would be assured—as well as being increased.

SUMMARY OF INCOME AND CAPITAL ADJUSTMENTS

	MAKE NO CHANGES	SELL THE STOCK OUTRIGHT	SELL THE STOCK USING A CRT
Lifetime spendable income for Jim and Betty	$198,720	$410,688	$485,720
Net benefit to the children	$270,000	$209,250	$275,000
Gift to the Sheltered Workshop	$ 0	$ 0	$600,000

To summarize, if the decision is to make no change, Jim and Betty will have a lifetime spendable income from this $600,000 of less than half of what they would have if the portfolio were restructured and reinvested.

Of the two remaining options—an outright sale of the stock or gifting the stock using a charitable remainder trust—the CRT option produces significantly better results for both Jim and Betty and the children. In fact, that option produces more than 18 percent greater income for Jim and Betty and almost one-third more inheritance for the children. And their favorite charity, the sheltered workshop, will get $600,000, instead of nothing.

6 Selling the Successful Business—Without the Tax Man

In our last chapter, when we visited with the Brewers and the Lincolns, we dealt directly with providing retirement income and the important role that solid planning can play. Since a concern about the adequacy of retirement income is the principal reason most people save, it deserves our attention. For that reason, we are going to look at two additional situations in which the need to provide an income for retirement was important but which was secondary to the sale of a successful business.

A large and growing number of people have spent their lives nurturing and tending a business, intending that it would, someday, provide for their retirement. Often, they are sorely disappointed when the time comes for them to sell the business and retire. They are disappointed, not because the business sold for so little, but because the tax man took so much. We are going to visit with Jim and Nancy Smith, and with a dynamic entrepreneur named Max Lyle, who faced this situation.

The Smiths

Thirty years ago, Jim and Nancy Smith started a small plastics factory. Jim had graduated from a good engineering school, and Nancy had spent several years as a supervisor for a large insurance company. While they readily admit they knew little about running a business, there was one thing that they both knew well: Neither wanted to spend any more time in corporate America. Operating on the leanest of budgets, they often wondered if they were going to make it. As a result of their hard work and long hours, however, they did make it, and now—at age sixty-one—they enjoy a combined income of $200,000, as well as substantial equity in their company.

Over the years they had begun wondering when they were going to retire. Each time they considered it, however, the conversation was put on hold as they handled one business crisis or another. Then, almost out of the blue, Jim received a call from the president of a much larger company, who wanted to meet with him. Jim had known the caller only slightly, even though they both belonged to the same manufacturer's association. So, it was with more than a little curiosity that Jim and Nancy agreed to meet with him.

With only the barest preamble, their visitor offered to buy their company for $3 million, $2 million for the stock and a $1 million consulting contract and noncompete agreement. Nancy could hardly believe it. Just like that they were going to be retired. However, having learned early in their business careers to rely on the judgment of financial professionals, they deferred their decision until they talked with their accountant. Wanting to accept the offer, they were eager to share their news with this man who was not only their trusted adviser but also their friend. They met with him the next morning.

The Smith's Challenge

Their accountant was pleased for them; actually, he was also relieved. He had often expressed his concern that they had not begun a pension plan, and he was not sure how they were going to afford to retire. He suggested they get right down to business, and Jim showed him the purchase and consulting contracts that had been drawn up.

The accountant told them they should have the contracts reviewed by their attorney, but he would crunch the numbers and have an evaluation of the offer for them later that same day. It was with a light heart that they left the accountant's office, agreeing to return at 3:00 that afternoon.

When they returned to his office, they were greeted with a big smile and a hearty "congratulations." From a financial perspective, the offer was a good one. "You need to be sure you understand the income tax implications, however," the accountant continued. Jim said he understood that some tax would have to be paid.

Jim was stunned when the accountant said the taxes would amount to just under $1 million. "How could that be?" Nancy asked. The accountant responded that, since the growth of their business was due largely to their own skill and hard work, they had almost no remaining cost basis in the company. As a result, the entire $2 million would be considered capital gains and subject to capital gains and state income taxes. In addition, the $1 million consulting contract would result in an additional $396,000 of ordinary income tax. "The actual total tax bill is likely to be about $936,000," the accountant concluded.

"This certainly puts a different light on the offer," Nancy observed. With the net sale proceeds at about $2 million after taxes, they would get about $160,000 a year in income. That wasn't bad, but it was a far cry from the $200,000 they had become used to. They agreed that they needed at least $190,000 of annual income to be comfortable, and that just wasn't going to happen by selling the company. Reluctantly, they told the buyer that his offer was refused.

About two months later, at a social gathering, they met a financial adviser. The conversation quickly turned to taxes, and Nancy recounted their recent disappointment. The adviser asked them if they had considered using the concept of social capital as a means of selling their business and avoiding the capital gains and income taxes on the profit. They said they were unfamiliar with the concept and asked for more information. The financial adviser suggested that they meet later the same week to discuss the matter more thoroughly.

When the day of the planned meeting arrived, the adviser outlined a hypothetical planning strategy—the actual plan would require some data gathering with the Smiths—that took advantage of the social capital concept he had discussed with them previously. The strategy involved using a charitable remainder trust into which Jim and Nancy would transfer their stock. The trust would sell the stock and provide an income to Jim and Nancy for the rest of their lives. When they died, the balance of the funds in the trust would pass to a charity they selected. Through another trust, their children would still receive a substantial inheritance.

Nancy and Jim agreed to give the adviser the personal and business information that he needed to develop a specific plan using the strategy that he had outlined. He suggested, however, that the Smiths let their accountant and attorney know he would be asking them to join him in developing their plan. They readily agreed.

The Smiths' Objectives

After meeting with the Smiths' other advisers to brief them on the approach he expected to take with their clients, the financial adviser again met with the Smiths to learn as much about their situation as he could.

At the end of a lengthy fact-finding meeting, the financial adviser had all the important information about the company and the Smiths that he needed, including their objectives—which were to

1. Sell their business with a minimum of tax

2. Generate an income of at least $190,000 each year

3. Leave a sizable charitable gift to the local hospital

4. Leave an inheritance of $1 million to their children

The adviser then made arrangements to meet with the attorney and accountant. Together they developed a plan that would allow the Smiths to sell their business and retire on the investment income that would result. The five-step plan took the following shape:

1. The Smiths would create a charitable remainder trust and name themselves as trustees in order to maintain the maximum control possible. They would then transfer all of their stock to the trust as a charitable contribution. As a result of the transfer, they would receive an income tax deduction amounting to $356,440.

2. They would appoint an independent trustee to sell the stock. Assuming the previous prospective purchaser continued to be interested in purchasing the company, the purchase would result in the charitable remainder trust's realizing $2 million to invest. The adviser pointed out to the Smiths that it was critical that neither the buyer nor seller be under any compulsion to buy or sell because of a prior agreement. If they were, that would jeopardize the tax advantages of the transaction.

3. The $2 million stock sale proceeds would be invested by the Smiths as trustees. As income beneficiaries of the trust, they would receive 8 percent each year of the trust principal. In their first year they would receive $160,000 and could receive more in later years, depending upon the balance in the trust. In addition, the consulting contract would pay them an additional $200,000 per year for the next five years, much of which could be invested to produce income in later years.

4. In order to fund a wealth replacement trust, the Smiths would contribute $22,000 each year for the next ten years to purchase $1 million of life insurance, which would be paid to their children upon the death of the last survivor of Jim and Nancy.

5. Also, upon the death of the last survivor, the local hospital would receive $2 million, which would be earmarked to help build the new Smith Eye Clinic.

If we outline and compare the tax and cash flow results coming from the two alternatives: the outright stock sale and the charitable remainder trust, we can begin to see the advantages of the charitable trust.

INVESTMENT ASSET ANALYSIS

	SELL THE STOCK OUTRIGHT	SELL THE STOCK USING A CRT
Value of the stock	$2,000,000	$2,000,000
less, the Smiths' cost basis	— 0	— 0
Capital gains realized on the stock sale	2,000,000	2,000,000
times, the state and federal tax rate	× 27%	× 0%
Sale proceeds	$2,000,000	$2,000,000
less, taxes to be paid on the stock sale	— 540,000	— 0
Assets available for investment	$1,460,000	$2,000,000

An important advantage that evolves from the use of the charitable remainder trust is the tax advantage. Although the gain resulting from the stock sale was identical whether sold outright or through the trust, the key issue was the rate at which that gain would be taxed. If the stock were sold outright, the gain would be included in the Smiths' income and taxed at the federal capital gains tax rate of 20 percent and state income tax rate of 7 percent. Alternatively, if the stock were sold through a charitable remainder trust, the gain would be included in the trust's income. However, since the charitable remainder trust is tax-exempt, it has a 0 percent tax rate. Since no capital gains or income taxes would be paid on a sale through the trust, the entire $2 million sale proceeds would be available to produce an income. At an 8 percent investment rate, the additional annual income resulting from the tax savings is $43,200. The entire $2 million, instead of $1.5 million, will provide income and enhance cash flow.

If we now look at the cash flow analysis, you will notice that the Smiths' lifetime spendable income has increased almost one third just by using the charitable remainder trust approach. What is very interesting is that this substantial increase in spendable income is *after* they have already replaced the asset by buying life insurance. So, the life insurance cost has already been accounted for.

	SELL THE STOCK OUTRIGHT	SELL THE STOCK USING A CRT
CASH FLOW ANALYSIS		
Annual gross income from investment*	$ 116,800	$ 160,000
Annual net income after 39.6% tax	70,547	96,640
times, the Smith's life expectancy	× 24	× 24
Lifetime net income	$1,693,128	$2,319,360
Charitable income tax deduction	0	349,538
times, the Smiths' income tax bracket	× 39.6%	× 39.6%
The Smiths' income tax savings	0	$ 138,417
Annual life insurance premium	0	22,000
times, number of years payable#	× 0	× 11
Total life insurance cost	0	242,000
Smiths' lifetime net income	$1,693,128	$2,319,360
plus, income tax savings	0	+ 138,417
less, total life insurance cost	0	− 242,000
Lifetime spendable income	$1,693,128	$2,215,777

*Based on an 8 percent investment return.

#Based on the current dividend scale which is not guaranteed.

Finally, if we look at the benefits passed to the children under both scenarios, we can see that, since the stock had been transferred to the charitable remainder trust, the entire value of the stock had been removed from the Smiths' taxable estate. However, since the stock would be passed to the hospital upon their death, it reduced the inheritance to the children by $657,000—the amount they would have received if the stock had been sold outright and the various income, capital gains, and estate taxes had been paid. To replace the stock value that had been contributed, the wealth replacement trust would pay the children $1 million, completely free of income or estate taxes.

ESTATE ANALYSIS

	SELL THE STOCK OUTRIGHT	SELL THE STOCK USING A CRT
Value of the asset in the taxable estate	$1,460,000	$ 0
times, the estate tax rate	× 55%	× 55%
Estate tax payable on the asset	803,000	0
Value of the asset in the taxable estate	$1,460,000	$ 0
less, the estate tax payable	− 803,000	− 0
Value of asset to the children	657,000	0
plus, life insurance to the children	+ 0	+ 1,000,000
Net benefit to the children	$ 657,000	$1,000,000

SUMMARY ANALYSIS

	SELL THE STOCK OUTRIGHT	SELL THE STOCK USING A CRT	PERCENT DIFFERENCE
Smith's lifetime spendable income	$1,693,128	$2,215,777	+ 30.9%
Children's inheritance	657,000	1,000,000	+ 52%
Smith Eye Clinic	0	2,000,000	!!!
Income, capital gains and estate taxes	1,343,000	0	!!!

In summarizing the strategy for the Smiths, the benefits of the charitable trust are the result of using a number of tax-advantaged techniques and products to multiply the effectiveness of what they are doing:

- Using a tax-exempt trust enabled the Smiths to liquidate their highly appreciated stock without any federal capital gains or state income tax result.

- Retaining the beneficial income interest while making a charitable gift of the remainder interest allowed them to enjoy the increased income from their liquidated stock and a substantial current income tax deduction.

- Making the charitable gift of the stock removed the asset from their estate for tax purposes.

- Using life insurance to replace the value of the asset permits them to leverage their costs to provide a substantially greater income tax-free death benefit since it may be unlikely that they would pay more than $.25 for each $1 paid in death benefits.

- Using an irrevocable wealth replacement trust allows them to pass that inheritance along to their children completely free of estate taxes.

Maxwell Lyle

When Max Lyle graduated from engineering school, he went from job to job, trying to find something that excited him. Unfortunately, none of the jobs did. It was his father's heart disease and Max's general curiosity about almost everything that changed his life. It led him to invent an important element of an artificial heart valve that became the beginning of Lyle Technology, Incorporated.

That was twenty-five years ago. Now age fifty-one and after twenty-five years of service to his community, Max Lyle has decided to sell Lyle Technology, the firm he founded and nurtured to success. His role in the company had changed, and he felt it was time to enter another phase of his life. He wouldn't retire, though. He was going to provide consulting services to other firms in his field for the next ten years or so. With the background of his own successful organization, it was generally acknowledged that he had a great deal to offer other entrepreneurs. First, however, he had to sell his own company.

Max expects that his company stock will sell for about $5 million and that it will cost him about $1.4 million in capital gains and state income taxes. As a result, he expects to net about $3.6 million from the sale, which he intends to invest. For the next ten years he will live off his consulting income while his investment earnings accumulate. At the end of the ten-year period, Max plans to retire and wants to be able to withdraw $1 million to purchase a yacht and to use for other personal enjoyment.

Max didn't want to pay almost a million and a half dollars in taxes, but he felt it was the best possible plan, considering the tax laws. Before he implemented his plan, however, he talked to a friend who suggested a different approach. After listening to what Max wanted to accomplish, his friend, a financial adviser, suggested using a tax-free trust.

Max's Objectives

Unlike the situations we reviewed earlier, Max had no interest in receiving income immediately. Since he would be consulting for ten years to the industry he knew so well, he felt he would have enough income during that time to meet his needs. His need for investment income would begin eleven years in the future.

Max listed his financial goals for his friend:

- Generate an after-tax spendable income of at least $350,000 each year, beginning in year eleven

- Build liquidity to $1 million as quickly as possible

- Have the flexibility and liquidity to withdraw large amounts of money during his life

- Leave an inheritance of $3.5 million

- Minimize the capital gains and income taxes on his company stock sale

- Leave a substantial charitable gift to his alma mater

The adviser suggested he consider a specially designed charitable remainder trust funded by a variable annuity. Using both of these products, he would be able to completely avoid taxes on the stock sale and regulate the flow of income to himself from the trust. Max was delighted that there was a way to sell the business without paying taxes and asked the financial adviser to proceed with the development of a plan that used these products.

Max's financial adviser met with his accountant and attorney to develop a plan that would meet his objectives. Here is the six-point plan they developed:

1. Max would establish a charitable remainder trust—a special CRT called a net income charitable remainder unitrust with an income make-up provision—and contribute his $5 million in company stock to it. He would name himself as trustee and, acting as such, would sell the stock. Since the trust is tax-exempt, no income or capital gains taxes would be paid on the gain.

2. The $5 million realized on the sale of the stock would be invested by Max into a specially designed variable annuity contract, which would allow the trustee—within limits—to start, stop, and limit income distributions to the trust as needed to meet the plan objectives.

3. A wealth replacement trust would be immediately established, which would apply for and own a $3.5 million life insurance policy on Max's life payable to Max's heirs. The benefit would be paid completely free of any tax.

4. The trust would distribute a net $55,000 each year for fifteen years to pay the premium for the $3.5 million life insurance policy in the wealth replacement trust.

5. The charitable remainder trust would make a lump-sum distribution of $1 million in year eleven for the purchase of the yacht and an additional $590,875 as income in that and the next four years. When funding of the life insurance policy ceased after year fifteen, an additional $92,000 of income would be paid to Max for each succeeding year.

6. Upon Max's death, a charitable gift of approximately $8.5 million would be made to the university where Max went to engineering school.

Max was delighted with the plan and implemented it immediately. Let's look at the various financial statements comparing the outright stock sale with the charitable remainder trust alternative.

INVESTMENT ASSET ANALYSIS

	SELL THE STOCK OUTRIGHT	SELL THE STOCK USING A CRT
Value of the stock	$5,000,000	$5,000,000
less, Max's cost basis	— 0	— 0
Capital gains realized on the stock sale	5,000,000	5,000,000
times, the capital gains and income tax rate	× 27%	× 0%
Taxes paid on the stock sale	1,350,000	0
Sale proceeds	$5,000,000	$5,000,000
less, taxes to be paid on the stock sale	— 1,350,000	— 0
Assets available for investment	$3,650,000	$5,000,000

The investment asset analysis is quite straightforward. If the stock were sold outright, capital gains and state income taxes of $1.35 million would have to be paid. Since the stock is gifted to a tax-exempt trust, no taxes are paid, even though the gain is the same. The net result, of course, is that the trust has an additional $1.35 million to invest.

CASH FLOW ANALYSIS

	SELL THE STOCK OUTRIGHT	SELL THE STOCK USING A CRT
Account balance after year 11*	$4,833,185	$8,535,935
Annual gross income at 8%	386,655	682,875
Annual net income in 40% tax bracket	231,993	409,725
times, Max's life expectancy after retirement	× 21	× 21
Lifetime net income	$4,871,853	$8,604,225
Charitable income tax deduction	0	$ 836,450
times, Max's income tax bracket	× 40%	× 40%
Income tax savings[v]	0	$ 334,580
Annual life insurance premium	0	$ 55,200
times, number of years payable[#]	0	× 15
Total life insurance cost	0	$ 828,000
Max's lifetime net income	$4,871,853	$8,604,225
plus, income tax savings	0	+ 334,580
less, total life insurance cost	0	− 828,000
Lifetime spendable income	$4,871,853	$8,110,805

* Annual earnings of 8 percent are compounded (after tax for the outright sale and tax-free in the CRT) until year eleven at which time $1 million is withdrawn.

[v] The actual income tax savings will depend upon the extent of other income since the deduction is limited to 30 percent of adjusted gross income with a 5 year carry-forward.

[#] Based on a crediting rate of 6.25 percent which is not guaranteed.

The comparative cash flow statement is dramatic. If Max were to sell his stock outright and invest the $3.65 million of after-tax proceeds in a taxable investment, he would have $4.83 million at the end of the eleventh year, assuming he withdrew the income tax due each year from the fund and withdrew the $1 million in year eleven. If he used the charitable remainder trust approach, the amount in the fund at the end of the eleventh year—after his $1 million withdrawal—would be $8.5 million, since he not only had more net investment proceeds in year one, but he was also not required to pay income taxes on the growth in the fund, since it was held in the tax-exempt trust.

Since the account balance was significantly higher in the trust, the income was also much greater. In fact, after adding the income tax savings and deducting the total life insurance premium cost, the lifetime spendable income resulting from the trust approach was 66 percent greater than it would have been if Max had sold the stock outright.

The only area that may be open to question is the extent of the income tax savings. The income tax savings of $334,580 is the total income tax deduction of $836,450 in Max's 40 percent income tax bracket. This may be overstated, depending upon the extent of Max's income, since the charitable deduction of appreciated property is limited to 30 percent of the donor's adjusted gross income and may be taken in the year in which the gift is made and any balance carried over to the five succeeding years. If Max's income was not sufficiently high, the actual deduction—and, correspondingly, the savings—could be lower. However, even if the entire deduction were disregarded, the trust income would, nonetheless, be more than 60 percent greater than the income derived from the outright stock sale. So, it makes a difference, but Max's decision would, nonetheless, have been the same.

The estate analysis showed a significantly greater benefit to Max's heirs.

ESTATE ANALYSIS

	SELL THE STOCK OUTRIGHT	SELL THE STOCK USING A CRT
Value of the asset in the taxable estate	$4,833,185	$ 0
times, the estate tax rate	× 55%	× 55%
Estate tax payable on the asset	$2,658,252	$ 0
Value of the asset in the taxable estate	$4,833,185	$ 0
less, the estate tax payable	− 2,658,252	0
Value of the asset to the heirs	$2,174,933	$ 0
plus, life insurance to the heirs	+ 0	+ 3,500,000
Net benefit to the heirs	$2,174,933	$3,500,000

The estate analysis illustrates that the benefits derived from the use of a charitable remainder trust are not limited to the income beneficiary. The additional $1.33 million in the tax-free benefit to the heirs represents a 61 percent greater inheritance.

The plain fact is that everyone benefited from Max's use of the charitable remainder trust. Not the least of the additional benefits was the $8.535 million charitable gift to the university. The comparative benefit summary statement looked like this:

SUMMARY ANALYSIS

	SELL THE STOCK OUTRIGHT	SELL THE STOCK USING A CRT
Max's lifetime spendable income	$4,871,853	$8,110,805
Benefits to the heirs	$2,174,933	$3,500,000
Contribution to the university	0	$8,535,935
Income, capital gains, and estate taxes	$4,008,252	$ 0

Is it any wonder that Max chose the charitable remainder trust option to maximize his capital—both his financial capital and his social capital?

7 Minimizing Estate Taxes on Substantial Estates

As we have seen in certain previous cases, the successful business—often built from the ground up by an enterprising entrepreneur—is both a testament to the hard work and intelligence of its founders and an enormous financial challenge when the entrepreneur wants to sell it and move on to something else. Frequently, the founder's investment has consisted principally of leadership, long hours, and insight—significant "costs," but difficult investments from which to establish a cost basis—rather than cash. As a result, a sale of the successful business can be a very taxing problem. The next couple we will visit—the Pearsons—faced exactly this problem.

The Pearsons

Joe and Shirley Pearson, both in their early sixties, own and manage a successful manufacturing company, which they estimate is worth about $4 million. When added to their personal investments, the house they own and their vacation condominium, their net worth is about $5 million. All three of their children are grown and have careers of their own. None of the children has shown any interest in managing the company.

Building and managing a family business requires a commitment in time, money, and energy equaled by few other endeavors. As a result, the time that Joe and Shirley spent with their three children was always too little and, they feared, sometimes too late. They now have four grandchildren and have decided that they are not willing to miss their grandchildren's lives as well. In addition, they are hoping to do all of the traveling and sightseeing that they have been putting off while the business flourished. In other words, they have concluded that it is time to sell the business.

In a meeting with their accountant in which they reviewed the likely tax issues that surround selling the business, it became clear that they needed to meet with an experienced financial adviser. At their request, their accountant arranged for them to meet with a registered investment adviser experienced in the valuation and sale of companies.

The adviser began by asking the Pearsons to state, in simple words, how they hoped to spend the rest of their life. They outlined their wish to sell their company, their travel plans, their intention to become better acquainted with their children and grandchildren and their desire to become more active in their church and the local children's hospital, which they credited with saving the life of one of their children. The adviser then inventoried their assets, arranged a time for their next meeting, and then asked Joe and Shirley what they expected from the planning process.

The Pearsons hope to

- Create a lifetime income that would increase over time to offset the erosion caused by inflation

- Minimize the taxes on their sale of the business

- Provide a substantial inheritance to each of their children

- Leave a significant gift to the children's hospital, rather than paying estate taxes

After the initial meeting with the Pearsons, the financial adviser met with the accountant, the Pearsons' attorney, and the local trust officer to form a planning team with the needed experience. Together, the planning team developed a plan that was presented to the Pearsons at their next meeting.

The Plan

The six-point plan developed by the team incorporated the following elements:

1. The Pearsons would establish a charitable remainder trust and name themselves as co-trustees in order to maintain the maximum control over the contributed assets. In addition, they would name the Pearson Charitable Family Foundation as the remainder beneficiary of the trust. An independent special trustee would be named with the sole authority to value the hard-to-value assets, such as the stock in the family company.

2. They would contribute 75 percent of their company stock to the charitable remainder trust; this contribution would create an immediate income tax deduction of $620,000, which Joe and Shirley could take in the current year and carry over into the next five years, as necessary. As trustees, they would sell the contributed stock with the intention of investing the assets to produce trust income. Since the trust is tax-exempt, no capital gains taxes would be payable upon the sale.

3. They would sell the remaining 25 percent of the stock outright to the purchaser of the earlier 75 percent of the stock.

4. The Pearsons would create an additional irrevocable trust called a "wealth replacement trust," through which they would arrange an inheritance for their children. This trust would purchase a $3 million life insurance policy that, since it would not be considered a part of the estate, would pass to the children completely free of either estate or income taxes. The premiums for this life insurance would be funded through the income tax savings generated by the charitable gift and the increased income generated by the charitable remainder trust.

5. Joe and Shirley would pass an additional $1.2 million outright to their children, the amount that could be passed estate tax free. The balance of the estate would be passed to the Pearson Charitable Family Foundation.

6. The Pearson's children would be named as salaried co-directors of the Pearson Charitable Family Foundation. As such, they would receive an annual salary from the foundation for their activities in directing its charitable activities.

After reviewing the various financial statements distributed during this meeting, the Pearsons directed their attorney to draft the necessary documents to implement the plan. The first statement was the investment asset analysis.

It was clear from the financial statement that, not considering the charitable deduction, the charitable remainder trust resulted in $810,000 more to invest for income. If all of the stock had been sold outright, the $4 million purchase price would have been reduced by the $1,080,000 needed to pay federal capital gains and state income taxes. By using the trust to sell $3 million of the stock, the taxes were limited to $270,000— still substantial, but considerably less than they might have been.

Because the net investment proceeds available were $810,000 greater, the additional annual income at 8 percent was $64,800. Over a possible twenty-five-year additional life span, the increase in total income could amount to more than $1.6 million. Just that fact, alone, could strongly suggest the use of a charitable remainder trust.

INVESTMENT ASSET ANALYSIS

	SELL ALL STOCK OUTRIGHT	SELL THE STOCK USING A CRT
Value of company stock	$4,000,000	$4,000,000
less, stock gifted to the CRT	– 0	– 3,000,000
Balance of stock sold outright	$4,000,000	$1,000,000
Stock sold outright	$4,000,000	$1,000,000
less, charitable deduction	0	618,500
less, Pearson's cost basis	– 0	– 0
Capital gains	$4,000,000	$ 381,490
Capital gains	$4,000,000	$ 381,490
times, income and capital gains tax rates*	× 27%	× 27%
Taxes payable on the sale	$1,080,000	$ 103,002
Sale proceeds	$4,000,000	$4,000,000
less taxes	– 1,080,000	– 103,002
Assets available to produce income	$2,920,000	$3,896,998

* Assuming a 20 percent federal capital gains tax rate and an average 7 percent state income tax rate.

If we look at the cash flow analysis, we can see that they could increase their lifetime spendable income by almost $350,000, or about 9 percent, by selling 75 percent of their company stock through the charitable remainder trust. They could increase their annual income another 10 percent by selling all of the stock through the trust. The trade-off, however, is that the children would receive a somewhat smaller inheritance.

CASH FLOW ANALYSIS

	SELL ALL STOCK OUTRIGHT	SELL THE STOCK USING A CRT
Annual gross income	$ 233,600	$ 311,760
times, income tax bracket	× 31%	× 31%
Income taxes	$ 72,416	$ 96,646
Annual gross income	$ 233,600	$ 311,760
less, income taxes	− 72,416	− 96,646
Annual after-tax income	$ 161,184	$ 215,114
less, annual insurance premium	− 0	− 40,000
Annual spendable income	$ 161,184	$ 175,114
times, life expectancy	× 25	× 25
Lifetime spendable net income	$4,029,600	$4,377,850

The increased income to the Pearsons made the charitable remainder trust attractive. Their overriding concern, however, was that their children not be disinherited because of their parents' charitable inclination and desire for additional income.

The estate analysis shows, however, that their children would inherit almost $1.6 million more by using the charitable remainder trust than if the Pearsons had sold the stock outright. By giving away their assets they would have more income and their children would have an almost 60 percent larger inheritance.

ESTATE ANALYSIS

	SELL ALL STOCK OUTRIGHT	SELL THE STOCK USING A CRT
After-tax stock sale proceeds	$2,920,000	$ 896,998
plus, other assets	+ 1,000,000	+ 1,000,000
Personally held assets	$3,920,000	$1,896,998
plus, charitable trust assets	+ 0	+ 3,000,000
Gross estate	$3,920,000	$4,896,998
Gross estate	$3,920,000	$4,896,998
less, charitable estate tax deduction	– 0	– 3,696,998
Taxable estate	$3,920,000	$1,200,000
less, estate taxes	– 1,264,907	– 0
Estate assets passed to children	$2,655,092	$1,200,000
plus, life insurance proceeds	+ 0	+ 3,000,000
Direct benefit to the children	$2,655,092	$4,200,000

SUMMARY ANALYSIS

	SELL ALL STOCK OUTRIGHT	SELL THE STOCK USING A CRT
Lifetime spendable income to Pearsons	$4,029,600	$4,377,850
Inheritance for the children	$2,655,092	$4,200,000
Pearson Charitable Family Foundation	0	$3,696,998

In addition to the obvious benefits of using a charitable remainder trust to sell appreciated property, there is an additional benefit that applies to private foundations like the one established by the Pearsons: the opportunity to provide meaningful employment—and substantial compensation—to their children and grandchildren.

A private foundation is required to distribute at least 5 percent of its assets each year. The balance of a foundation's earnings can go to legitimate expenses, including salaries for descendants who provide services to the foundation. For example, if the Pearsons' foundation remains at its current size and produces 8 percent income in a given year, that amounts to $295,760. If the foundation distributes 5 percent of its assets, it would give away $184,850. That leaves $110,910 that can provide salaries for descendants.

In this case, everyone clearly won. The Pearsons increased their income and the inheritance for their children, and in the process, they created the family foundation, which could provide employment for their children and grandchildren.

8 Diversifying the Appreciated Portfolio—Without Taxes

Nothing is so certain as change; we need only look around us. Some of the industrial and retailing giants of just a few years ago are little more than memories. As tastes evolve and technological advances change the face of business, the small, agile David continues to slay the monolithic Goliath. But the world continues to evolve, and David eventually falls victim to demographics, technology, and consumer preference.

For the investor, one of the big challenges is to avoid personal financial disaster when a company's prospects suddenly dim and its preeminent position is lost. The means to avoiding that kind of debacle lie in diversification, the process of distributing investments among various companies, sectors, etc., in order to reduce overall portfolio risk. The problem in diversifying the successful portfolio, however, is often the investor's need to recognize the capital gains resulting when highly appreciated stock is sold to make room for other securities required to implement the diversification strategy. Although the simultaneous sale of the portfolio's securities that will generate a capital loss to offset the gain can sometimes be used effectively, that is not often an available strategy when the appreciated security is the result of the exercise of stock options and company stock makes up the majority of the portfolio.

In our next case history, we will meet someone facing exactly this kind of challenge.

Joan Lerner

Joan Lerner is vice president of computer engineering for a rapidly growing Silicon Valley computer hardware and software firm. Her firm's exploitation of the potential of a unique market niche has resulted in a meteoric rise in the company's stock. Her incentive stock options, which allowed her to purchase company stock for the price that it had when the options were given to her, have, as a result, increased her net worth dramatically.

She must hold the options for at least two years to avoid recognizing income when she exercises the options. In addition, she needs to keep the stock for the required holding period to qualify for a more favorable long-term capital gains tax rate on any profit resulting from its sale. Joan was concerned that, despite her firm's rapid historic growth, its hold on market share may erode, resulting in a plummeting stock price. Even if that never happened, she just isn't comfortable tying her personal fortunes to the vagaries of a single company. Her company is thriving today, but some of the best-managed companies in Silicon Valley and elsewhere have gone bust, taking their stockholders with them. Diversifying her stock portfolio—currently containing only company stock—is vital. She knows what needs to be done; her concern is that in doing it she will be turning a large part of her retirement dollars into tax dollars.

Although a sale of the company stock after the required holding period would afford Joan the more favorable capital gains tax rate, her extremely low cost basis would mean that almost all of the proceeds from the sale would be profit. Not knowing how to proceed, she called her CPA to get some advice. He suggested she meet with a financial adviser who specializes in tax issues involving the sale of property.

Joan's Objectives

The meeting began with the adviser explaining the process involved in the development of a financial plan. Beginning with a thorough understanding of Joan's objectives, resulting from a data-gathering session, he would meet with a team of legal and financial advisers, including Joan's attorney and accountant, to create a preliminary plan for her review. After her review of the plan—which would include an analysis of options available to her—any desired changes would be made. Her attorney would then draft the documents, and the plan would be implemented in accordance with a step-by-step schedule designed to meet any legal and tax requirements.

Joan detailed her objectives for the adviser. She had four primary objectives that the plan needed to satisfactorily address.

The plan needed to:

- Accumulate funds during her remaining working years

- Provide an annual income flow of at least $120,000 that would begin at her retirement and last for the remainder of her life, which she could increase or decrease as needed

- Leave an inheritance to her daughter of $1 million

- Provide for the diversifying of her existing assets in the most tax-smart way possible

Although Joan had not considered any charitable bequests, she felt a particular closeness to her alma mater, a local university just north of Silicon Valley.

Joan's Plan

Any plan developed needs to be evaluated in light of the existing options available to accomplish the same task. Because of that, two plans were developed; one plan called for Joan to hold the company stock for the required holding period and then sell it, diversifying the portfolio through the purchase of other securities. The second plan called for the transfer of the stock to a charitable trust, which would sell the stock and purchase other securities.

In the second plan, the stock transferred to the trust would eventually go to a charity. A wealth replacement trust would provide an inheritance to Joan's daughter. By implementing this second plan, Joan's retirement income increased by more than 50 percent, and her daughter received a 10 percent larger inheritance.

According to the alternative five-point plan developed by the planning team, the following steps would need to be taken to accomplish the objectives:

1. Joan would establish a special charitable remainder trust, referred to as a Net Income Charitable Remainder Unitrust with Makeup Option (NIMCRUT), and name herself as trustee in order to maintain asset control, giving sole authority to value and make investment decisions concerning Joan's stock to an independent special trustee.

2. Joan would continue to exercise her stock options and, after satisfying the one-year holding period, would contribute $100,000 worth of stock to the trust in each of ten years; she would obtain a $330,000 income tax deduction for the contributions.

3. The trust would sell the stock and invest the funds in a diversified investment portfolio using a specially designed deferred variable annuity.

4. Joan would establish a second irrevocable trust, called a "wealth replacement trust," which would purchase and own a $1 million life insurance policy on her life; the policy would be personally paid for by Joan, partly with funds resulting from income tax savings she would derive as a result of her stock contributions.

5. Upon Joan's death, her daughter would receive $1 million tax free, and her alma mater would receive a gift projected to be approximately $2.9 million.

This plan would result in Joan's receiving 55 percent more retirement income. Let's begin with an analysis of the retirement capital itself and how it would be derived.

INVESTMENT ASSET ANALYSIS

	SELL THE STOCK OUTRIGHT	SELL THE STOCK USING A CRT
Value of stock purchased by annual stock option exercise	$ 100,000	$ 100,000
times, number of years exercised	× 10	× 10
Total value of stock received	$1,000,000	$1,000,000
Total value of stock sold	$1,000,000	$1,000,000
less, Joan's cost basis	− 0	− 0
Capital gain realized on sale of the stock	$1,000,000	$1,000,000
Capital gain realized	$1,000,000	$1,000,000
times, capital gains and income tax rates*	× 27%	× 0%
Capital gains tax payable	$ 270,000	$ 0
Stock value sold	$1,000,000	$1,000,000
less, capital gains tax payable	− 270,000	− 0
Net capital available for investment	$ 730,000	$1,000,000

* Assuming a federal capital gains tax rate of 20 percent and a state income tax rate of 7 percent.

The investment asset analysis is fairly straightforward, even for someone with limited financial background. Since the trust was tax-exempt, no capital gains or income taxes were payable upon its sale of the stock. As a result, it had the entire $1 million to invest instead of only $730,000. So far, so good.

We know the extent of the investment we have to work with in the case of each alternative. Let's see where that takes her in terms of income.

CASH FLOW ANALYSIS

	SELL THE STOCK OUTRIGHT	SELL THE STOCK USING A CRT
Capital available at Joan's age sixty-five	$1,835,871	$2,919,998
Gross annual retirement income*	$ 146,870	$ 233,600
times, income tax rate	× 40%	× 40%
Income tax payable	$ 58,748	$ 93,440
Gross annual retirement income	$ 146,870	$ 233,600
less, income tax payable	− 58,748	− 93,440
Annual net retirement income	$ 88,122	$ 140,160
Annual net retirement income	$ 88,122	$ 140,160
times, life expectancy at retirement	× 18	× 18
Total lifetime retirement income	$1,586,196	$2,522,880
Charitable income tax deduction	0	$ 331,754
times, Joan's income tax bracket	× 40%	× 40%
Income tax savings	0	$ 132,701
Total lifetime retirement income	$1,586,196	$2,522,880
less, life insurance premiums paid	− 0	− 196,734
plus, income tax savings	+ 0	+ 132,702
Total lifetime net spendable income	$1,586,196	$2,458,847

* Based on 8 percent annual return.

The income results are clear. By selling the stock, paying the capital gains and income taxes and reinvesting the remainder, she could expect to have a net annual retirement income at age sixty-five of about $88,000; by using the charitable remainder trust, that net annual income jumped to about $140,000. There are some adjustments to that income—specifically, life insurance premiums and a charitable deduction—but the lifetime result was still 55 percent greater with the charitable trust arrangement.

Of course, the capital that would be available at Joan's retirement, if she sold the stock outright, would be $1.8 million. Under the trust arrangement, her daughter would receive only $1 million. A $1 million dollar inheritance is not insignificant, but Joan was concerned that her daughter would have to have a reduced inheritance because of Joan's planning.

ESTATE ANALYSIS

	SELL THE STOCK OUTRIGHT	SELL THE STOCK USING A CRT
Value of the stock in Joan's taxable estate	$1,835,871	$ 0
times, the estate tax rate	× 50%	× 50%
Estate tax payable	$ 917,935	$ 0
Value of the stock in Joan's taxable estate	$1,835,871	$ 0
less, the estate tax payable	− 917,935	− 0
Value of the stock to Joan's daughter	$ 917,936	$ 0
Value of the stock to Joan's daughter	$ 917,936	$ 0
plus, the life insurance proceeds	+ 0	+ 1,000,000
Total assets to Joan's daughter	$ 917,936	$1,000,000

The estate analysis shows that, after taxes, the amount inherited by Joan's daughter is actually about nine percent greater using the trusts. That amount can be increased, of course, by increasing the life insurance owned by the wealth replacement trust. The trade-off for Joan would be a slightly reduced lifetime spendable income, when compared to the alternative plan, but still substantially more than if she had sold the stock outright.

SUMMARY ANALYSIS

	SELL THE STOCK OUTRIGHT	SELL THE STOCK USING A CRT
Joan's lifetime spendable income	$1,586,196	$2,458,847
Joan's daughter's inheritance	$ 917,936	$1,000,000
Joan's charitable gift to her alma mater	$ 0	$2,919,998
Estate and capital gains taxes paid	$1,481,278	$ 0

9 Your Retirement Plan— A Great Way to Accumulate, A Terrible Way to Distribute

Almost everyone will readily acknowledge that qualified retirement plans—pension plans, profit-sharing plans, 401(k) plans—are great methods for accumulating capital. The deposits are usually income tax deductible, and they grow on a tax-deferred basis. Not only does a participant's or employer's entire contribution, undiminished by taxes, find its way into the participant's account, but the money that would normally have been paid in income taxes is available to produce additional income. When qualified plans are criticized—and some sophisticated financial advisers do criticize them—they are not criticized because they fail to effectively accumulate money. The criticism is normally directed to the enormous tax problems that may occur when the funds are withdrawn.

Theresa Grant, the next client that we will visit, learned just how appropriate that criticism was.

Theresa Grant

Theresa Grant is seventy years old and has been a widow for the last two years. She has a small pension and income from a portfolio of securities. Her standard of living is quite modest, despite being left with, among other assets, a $1 million stock portfolio and a $1 million IRA account. In fact, she has just learned that she will have to take minimum distributions from her IRA next year, an account she has avoided invading, hoping to leave it to her two sons.

If she takes only the required minimum distribution each year and the account continues growing at its current rate, the IRA balance is likely to be fairly substantial at her death. Yet, as a result of various taxes that will be levied—income taxes and estate taxes—her two sons can expect to receive only about one third of the value of the IRA. Furthermore, her accountant has told her that there is no way that she can transfer a significant portion of the IRA funds to her children during her life without incurring substantial taxes.

Mrs. Grant had been a music student many years ago and had taught music throughout her career. She continues to be an active member of the symphony society and is concerned about furthering music students' education. Her other concern is her two adult sons. One of her sons is a fifty-year-old professional and is financially secure. The other is a forty-five-year-old spendthrift who has never experienced much financial success. It is clear to her that her children have vastly different financial needs.

She has arranged to meet with her accountant, specifically to deal with the problem of what to do with her IRA. The thought of 70 percent of it being taken in taxes is appalling to her. At the meeting, her accountant suggests that the IRA can be used to benefit both the symphony and her children by using a charitable remainder trust. He suggests that two charitable remainder trusts be established and that each be the beneficiary of 50 percent of the IRA upon her death. Her two sons would be the income beneficiaries of their individual trusts during their lifetimes, and at their death, the balance in the trusts would be passed to the symphony.

The accountant also suggested that she establish a wealth replacement trust, which would apply for and own a life insurance policy on her life designed to pay the taxes that will be due on the IRA's distribution at her death, without itself being the cause for payment of additional taxes. Since Mrs. Grant had not seen the IRA as a source of income for herself and yet was required to take withdrawals from it, those withdrawals could be used to pay the premium on the life insurance policy.

The two charitable remainder trusts could be designed to meet the particular needs of the two sons. For the financially successful son, the charitable remainder trust would be designed as a net income with a make-up charitable remainder unitrust—designated a NIMCRUT—which, when funded by a variable annuity, would allow him to accumulate the funds in the trust until retirement, if he chose, rather than begin receiving them immediately. For the financially troubled son, whose need is for both current income and for protection from his spendthrift habits, the charitable remainder trust would simply provide him with a lifetime income paid on a quarterly basis—with no latitude given to change the amount or timing of the payments.

Theresa Grant's Plan

According to the plan the accountant designed, the following steps would be taken:

1. She would recast her will to provide for the creation of two charitable remainder trusts to be established upon her death and designate each trust as a 50 percent beneficiary of the individual retirement account.

2. She would begin to take required minimum distributions from her IRA—as, by law, she must—and use a part of the net income to pay for the life insurance owned by an irrevocable trust, which would be earmarked to pay the estate taxes due and provide a small lump sum to her two sons.

3. Upon her death, each of her sons' charitable remainder trusts would be funded with 50 percent of the IRA and they would begin to receive their lifetime income, the financially secure son to accumulate the money and the spendthrift son to receive it outright.

4. Upon the death of each son, the balance of the charitable remainder trust would be passed to the scholarship fund of the Symphony Society.

CASH FLOW ANALYSIS

	WITHOUT THE CRT	WITH THE CRT
Income from the IRA	$1,081,097	$1,081,097
less, income tax at 39.6%	− 428,114	− 428,114
less, insurance premiums	− 0	− 115,995
Mrs. Grant's lifetime net spendable income	$ 652,983	$ 536,988

Unlike the more typical case of charitable remainder trust use, the cash flow analysis in this case demonstrates that the income beneficiary—Theresa Grant—will have less lifetime spendable income under the CRT plan. In Theresa Grant's case, the problem was not how to increase her income. In fact, she had not intended to use the IRA to provide income at all. Instead, the problem was how to transfer the funds to her sons and make a charitable gift. So, while a reduction in the income beneficiary's income would be unusual—and, very likely, unacceptable—in the normal case, it was a quite acceptable result in this case.

The more important financial statement for Mrs. Grant is the estate analysis, since it details the taxes payable and the income and asset flows at her death.

ESTATE ANALYSIS

	WITHOUT THE CRT	WITH THE CRT		
		TOTAL	SON 1	SON 2
Balance in the IRA	$798,091	$798,091		
IRA CRT contributions	0	798,091	399,046	399,045
less, charitable deduction —	0	− 178,693	− 66,956	− 111,737
Taxable estate	798,091	619,398	322,090	287,308
Taxable estate	798,091	619,398	322,090	287,308
less, estate taxes at 50%	− 399,046	− 309,699	− 166,045	− 143,654
Income in respect of				
a decedent	399,046	309,699	166,045	143,654
Income in respect of				
a decedent	399,046	309,699	166,045	143,654
times, income tax bracket	× 39.6% ×	0% ×	0% ×	0%
Income tax due*	158,022	0	0	0
Balance in IRA at death	798,091	798,091	399,046	399,045
less, contribution —	0	− 798,091	− 399,046	− 399,045
less, estate taxes	− 399,046	− 309,699	− 166,045	− 143,654
less, income taxes	− 158,022 —	0 —	0 —	0
plus, life insurance +	0	+ 350,000	+ 175,000	+ 175,000
lump sum balance to sons	241,023	40,301	8,955	31,346
CRT income to sons	0	2,033,896	1,258,236	775,660
less, income tax at 39.6% —	0	− 805,422	− 498,261	− 307,161
Sons' spendable income	0	1,228,474	759,975	468,499
plus, lump sum benefits + 241,023	+ 40,301	+ 8,955	+ 31,346
Total benefit to sons	241,023	1,268,775	768,930	499,845

* Income tax on income in respect of a decedent (IRD) is paid by the recipient. Since the charitable remainder trusts, the recipients under the CRT plan, are tax-exempt, no income tax is payable.

As the statement shows, her sons would have received a total of $241,023 from the IRA at their mother's death. Instead, because of the charitable remainder trust and the life insurance, they will receive a total of $1.26 million, more than five times the original amount.

The final statement was the summary analysis, providing the following information:

SUMMARY ANALYSIS		
	WITHOUT THE CRT	WITH THE CRT
Spendable income to Theresa Grant	$652,983	$ 536,988
After-tax benefit to the sons	$241,023	$1,268,775
Benefit to the Symphony	0	$ 992,006
Taxes paid	$557,068	$ 309,699

The final table recaps the comparative benefits of the two plans. Although Mrs. Grant's IRA spendable income declined slightly under the CRT plan, her two primary objectives—transferring the IRA benefit to her sons and benefiting the symphony—were both accomplished.

10 Investing Additional Spendable Income

It is often difficult to decide where to invest or save sudden increases in spendable income. There are so many choices, yet so often they involve significant risks to the investor's money. The decision is made even more complicated when the potential investor is motivated by a desire to benefit society while maximizing his or her assets. In our next case study, we will look at just such a situation.

The Wilburs

Dr. George Wilbur is a fifty-year-old physician with a successful private practice. He and his wife, Janet, age forty-eight, have just made the final mortgage payment on their house and are wrestling with the decision of where to put that additional $2,500 each month. Although George has been contributing to his pension plan regularly, he and Janet are concerned that the income it will provide won't be sufficient to support them after retirement.

George and Janet are both active in their community and have been strong supporters of charitable causes for many years. Janet has worked with and supported an organization providing educational and other opportunities to inner-city youths. Dr. Wilbur's charity has been directed principally to the hospital foundation. Their only child, a daughter, is approaching the end of medical school, so that expense is nearly over.

They have considered several investment possibilities, and have leaned towards a variable annuity. They like the idea of being able to invest their money in a number of separate accounts and believe that the deferral of income taxes on the growth can make a real difference in what they are able to accumulate. Still unsure about their choice, however, Dr. Wilbur attended a luncheon sponsored by the hospital foundation at which a financial adviser was scheduled to speak on "Maximizing Personal Assets Through Philanthropy."

The speaker talked about using a charitable remainder trust to increase assets and enjoy some tax advantages, while providing for the needs of the hospital foundation. George was intrigued and scheduled an appointment with the adviser to learn more about the idea.

The Wilburs' Objectives

At their meeting with the financial adviser, they discussed their situation and told him about their interest in a variable annuity to increase retirement income and their additional desire to make several charitable gifts. During a lengthy fact-finding session, they outlined their four primary financial objectives. Those objectives were to:

1. Create an additional source of retirement income that they could increase or decrease as they needed

2. Obtain any tax advantages possible in order to preserve additional cash to invest for retirement rather than pay taxes

3. Fund an endowment of $900,000 to benefit several charities

4. Provide at least as much inheritance to their daughter as she would have received if they had not made charitable gifts

At the end of the session, the adviser scheduled another appointment for one week hence to discuss an approach to meeting their objectives using a charitable remainder trust.

The Plan

Based on the extensive fact-finding, the adviser drew up a five-point plan designed to maximize the Wilburs' retirement income and its flexibility while providing significant benefits to their daughter and their charities. The adviser explained that the use of a NIMCRUT[14] could be much more advantageous than a variable annuity purchased outright.

---

[14] The Taxpayer Relief Act of 1997 increased the deductibility requirement from 5 percent to 10 percent for a charitable trust; this is a particularly important issue with the generally higher payout percentages of a NIMCRUT.

This was the broad outline of the plan:

1. The Wilburs would establish two trusts: a charitable remainder trust and a wealth replacement trust. They would name themselves trustees of the charitable remainder trust in order to maintain control over the assets. The charitable remainder trust would provide income to them and an eventual charitable gift while the wealth replacement trust would ensure that their daughter received an inheritance at least equal to the value of the asset she would have received if there had been no gift.

2. For the next eight years, they would divide the $30,000 annual trust contribution between the two trusts. The charitable remainder trust would receive $23,235; the wealth replacement trust would receive $6,765, which would be used to purchase life insurance payable to their daughter. At the end of the eight-year period, no further contributions would be made to the wealth replacement trust, and all further annual contributions—which would continue until Dr. Wilbur retired at age sixty-five—would be made to the charitable remainder trust.

3. Each contribution made to the charitable remainder trust would create a current income tax deduction that could be taken in the year in which the contribution was made, with any excess being carried over to the five subsequent years. The charitable remainder trust would invest the contributions in a variable annuity in order to produce significant appreciation coupled with an ability to avoid distribution in those years—principally during George's working years—when additional income would be unneeded and the additional tax unwanted.

4. At retirement, the Wilburs would receive a supplemental retirement income—adjustable as needed—for as long as either of them is living.

5. Upon the death of the last survivor of George and Janet, significant gifts would be made to the hospital foundation and to the inner-city youth program. In addition, the Wilburs' daughter would receive a fully tax-free death benefit from the wealth replacement trust at least equal to what she would have received if no gift had ever been made.

As you can see, the proposed plan accomplishes all of the Wilburs' objectives. Let's take a closer look at the details.

CAPITAL ANALYSIS

	ANNUITY PURCHASED OUTRIGHT	THE CRT PLAN
Annual retirement savings contributions:		
Years 1–8	$ 30,000	$ 23,235
Years 9–15	30,000	30,000
Total contributions	$450,000	$395,880
Annual wealth replacement costs:		
Years 1–8*	$ 0	$ 6,765
Total wealth replacement costs*	$ 0	$ 54,120
Total retirement savings contributions	$450,000	$395,880
plus, total wealth replacement costs	+ 0	+ 54,120
Total contributions	$450,000	$450,000

* Amount shown is based on the current dividend schedule and is not guaranteed

The capital analysis shows that over the next fifteen years, until his retirement at age sixty-five, Dr. Wilbur would be contributing a total of $395,880 to the charitable remainder trust and paying $54,120—the balance of the $450,000 total investment—for life insurance owned by the wealth replacement trust. So, whether George and Janet choose the variable annuity investment outright or the charitable remainder trust, their total outgo would be the same—$450,000.

INCOME ANALYSIS		
	ANNUITY PURCHASED OUTRIGHT	THE CRT PLAN
Total gross income during retirement	$2,047,366	$2,047,366
less, income tax at 31%	− 634,683	− 634,683
Net income	$1,412,683	$1,412,683
plus, charitable deduction tax savings	+ 0	+ 17,826
Total income	$1,412,683	$1,430,509

The income that Dr. and Mrs. Wilbur would derive from either option, as shown in the income analysis, would be the same. The total income would be slightly higher using the charitable remainder trust approach, since the charitable deductions would result in approximately $18,000 in income tax savings.

Assuming that the survivor of George and Janet lived for nineteen years after retirement, the projected income the couple would receive from this supplemental retirement savings program is presented graphically as shown below:

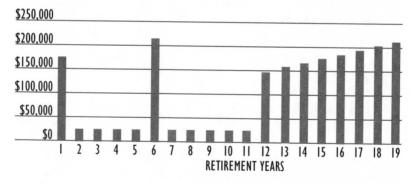

The projected income flow assumes the charitable remainder trust provides:

- A supplemental $25,000 per year to augment Dr. Wilbur's $100,000 pension plan withdrawal in years one through ten

- A lump sum of $175,000 in the first year to purchase a motor home

- An additional $190,000 in the sixth year for an upscale retirement community entrance fee

- $150,000 beginning in year twelve and increased by a compound 5 percent in each succeeding year until the assumed death of the survivor at the end of year nineteen

Based on this post-retirement cash flow, the remaining value of the charitable remainder trust (assuming a consistent 10 percent average annual net return) at the assumed death of the survivor would be $916,843. Let's turn our attention now to the asset flow at death as presented in the third table, the estate analysis.

ESTATE ANALYSIS

	ANNUITY PURCHASED OUTRIGHT	THE CRT PLAN
Income in respect of a decedent#	$1,481,082	$ 0
times, income tax rate	× 31%	× 0%
Income tax liability*	$ 459,135	$ 0
Value of the asset	$1,931,082	$916,843
less, charitable deduction	− 0	− 916,843
less, income tax liability	− 459,135	− 0
Taxable estate asset	$1,471,947	$ 0
Taxable estate asset	$1,471,947	$ 0
times, estate tax rate	× 50%	× 0%
Estate tax payable	$ 735,973	$ 0
Value of the asset	$1,931,082	$916,843
less, income taxes	− 459,135	− 0
less, charitable gift	− 0	− 916,843
less, estate taxes	− 735,973	− 0
Estate asset to daughter	$ 735,974	$ 0
plus, life insurance proceeds	+ 0	$750,000
Total asset to daughter	$ 735,974	$750,000

Income in respect of a decedent (IRD) in a variable annuity is the account value of the annuity less the remaining original cost basis. Annuities do not enjoy a step up in basis.

* Income tax on income in respect of a decedent is paid by the recipient. Since the charitable remainder trust is tax-exempt, no income tax is payable.

The asset that the Wilburs' daughter would receive in lieu of the variable annuity contract funds would consist of life insurance proceeds received completely tax free. If the Wilburs had chosen, the amount passed to their daughter could have been significantly increased simply by increasing the life insurance owned by the wealth replacement trust. The trade-off would have been a somewhat reduced charitable gift. As arranged in the plan and as detailed in the financial statement, the life insurance proceeds were about 2 percent greater than the funds their daughter would have received—after estate and income taxes were paid—if the Wilburs had never arranged for the gift.

The summary of the benefits is as follows:

SUMMARY ANALYSIS		
	ANNUITY PURCHASED OUTRIGHT	THE CRT PLAN
Retirement income to the Wilburs	$1,412,683	$1,430,509
The daughter's inheritance	$ 735,973	$ 750,000
Combined gifts to the hospital and youth center	0	$ 916,843
Combined taxes paid	$1,829,791	$ 634,683

It is clear from the summary analysis that the Wilburs have a means of maximizing their income and leaving a meaningful gift behind them, without affecting their daughter's inheritance.

11 Avoiding Double-Dose Taxes on Qualified Plans

The benefits to be found in qualified plans—pension, profit-sharing, 403(b), 401(k), IRAs and IRA rollovers—are compelling. They offer a current income tax deduction, a deferral of income taxes on the plan's earnings, and, generally, the plan's assets are sheltered from creditors. Not a bad array of benefits. Certainly, company- or practice-sponsored qualified plans require that you provide for other employees, which represents a cost. Generally, however, a qualified plan is an excellent way of accumulating assets.

There are few benefits that aren't accompanied by drawbacks; qualified plans are no exception. In fact, qualified plan penalties seem to be everywhere you turn. You will pay extra taxes if you take your qualified plan benefit too soon—or too late—or if you take too little! And, these penalties may be substantial. In the case of failing to take at least a minimum required distribution at age seventy and one half or older, the penalty is 50 percent of the amount you should have taken but didn't.

As though these penalties were not enough, the entire qualified plan assets are subject to a "double-dose" tax: a combination of estate taxes of up to 55 percent and state and federal income taxes (remember, you haven't paid income tax on these assets) of up to 40 percent of the net account balance after estate taxes. The total of these two taxes may exceed 70 percent of the account balance at your death. You can minimize these double-dose death taxes, and you can maximize the assets transferred to your heirs. We are going to introduce you to a pension distribution strategy that, in addition to providing the benefits to which we just alluded, offers two additional benefits:

- Since the strategy is revocable until you die, you may revise it or terminate it at any time

- The strategy will not affect your retirement plan during your lifetime.

As a means of examining this strategy, let's get to know Joe and Evie Cass. Joe is a sixty-year-old consulting engineer who is thinking seriously of retirement in the next two years, and fifty-eight-year-old Evie is his wife of thirty-five years. They have two children, Sarah and Ben, ages thirty and thirty-three, respectively.

Joe and Evie Cass

Joe Cass has been a consulting engineer for over thirty years. During that time, he has regularly added funds to his retirement program so that his vested account balance is now $1.5 million. Although Joe and Evie's income in retirement won't come close to their current income, they feel—since their mortgage is paid and their children are educated—that they can live comfortably.

Recently, Joe has begun hearing stories told by colleagues about tax problems having to do with their retirement plans. Rather than worry about it, however, Joe has made an appointment for the two of them to visit with a financial adviser to find out just what kind of tax problems they can expect.

The adviser explained that determining the extent of Joe and Evie's tax problem, if there was any, would require a full data-gathering session. However, there were certain general concerns that they might have about taxes and their pension plan.

Problems with Qualified Plans

One of the more odious taxes that people with substantial balances in their pension plans faced has just been repealed. It was known as the "success tax." This was a 15 percent penalty tax imposed on pension distributions that exceeded a certain amount.

Pension balances could still face significant tax erosion from both income and estate taxes, however, depending upon the extent of the pension participant's other assets. In fact, the tax drain could exceed 70 percent.

At the death of the participant of a qualified plan with a substantial balance, the pension funds are usually placed into a rollover IRA that, subsequently, provides an income to a surviving spouse. The big tax problems often arise at the death of the surviving spouse.

Value of Plan	$1,500,000
× Estate tax rate	× 45.3%
Estate tax due	$ 680,000
Balance subject to income tax	$ 820,000
× Income tax rate	× 40%
Income tax due	$ 328,000
Total tax due	$1,008,000

The fundamental problem is that two very significant taxes are levied against the plan balance. The first is an estate tax which could be as high as 55 percent. The second is an income tax, which, in the Cass's case, is about 40 percent. Graphically, their pension account balance is divided like this:

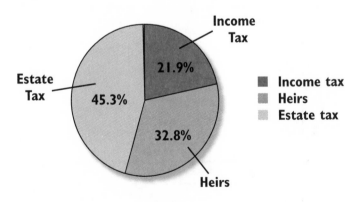

Although the graph shows that their children might only get about 33 percent of the pension balance that is left when the Casses die, actually, they could get even less. We'll look more closely at this when we look at the plan their adviser developed.

Joe and Evie's Current Plan

When we look at the transfer of wealth through wills and trusts, it is usually helpful to try to form a picture of it. So, what I'm going to do is to graphically take you through the process of transferring the Cass's assets at death, step by step.

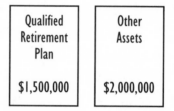

These two boxes represent their current assets. The assets in the box marked "Other Assets" include their residence, investment portfolio, vacation house, and so forth. The "Qualified Retirement Plan" box contains their vested accrued pension benefit.

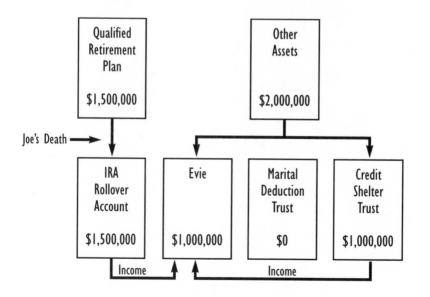

If Joe dies first, their assets outside of their qualified plan would be split. Half would go directly to Evie; half would be placed in a credit shelter trust. Any income earned by the assets in the trust would be paid to her.

Joe's qualified plan assets would probably be placed in an IRA rollover account in order to avoid having to pay income taxes on the entire account balance upon his death. This, too, would provide an income for Evie.

So far, the survivor will have been able to avoid taxes on the assets. The problem becomes acute when Evie dies.

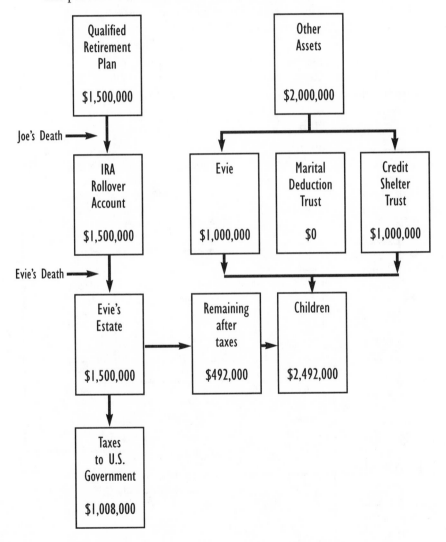

Upon Evie's death, their remaining current assets outside of their qualified retirement plan would pass to their children tax free. The $1 million that had passed to Evie outright could be passed to the children also tax free, assuming Evie lived to at least 2006, because of the unified credit given to everyone. The other half—the $1 million in the credit shelter trust—would not even be a part of Evie's estate, since she never owned the assets in the trust. The problem arises when we deal with the qualified plan assets.

As you can see, taxes take more than $1 million of the $1.5 million that was in the IRA rollover account. Under the Cass's current plan, only 32.8 percent of those assets pass to the children. They can reduce the amount of taxes to be paid and increase the amount passed to their children through a "pension optimal plan"—which would also create a substantial gift to their favorite charity or charities.

Pension Optimal Plan

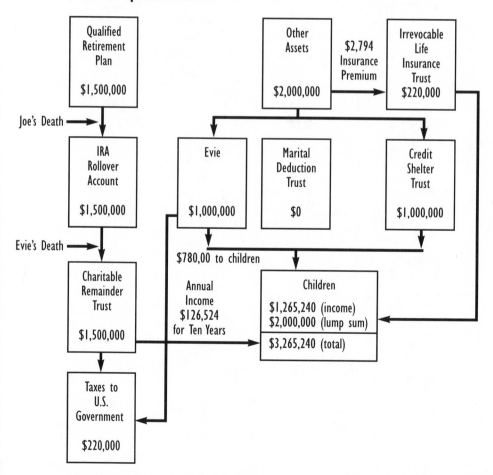

Let's begin with why you might want to consider this approach. Then I will explain how and why it accomplishes what it does.

Compared to the Cass's current plan, the pension optimal plan resulted in:

- A reduction in estate and income taxes from $1,008,000 to $220,000

- A change in the qualified plan assets to the children from a lump sum of $492,000 to a ten-year income of $126,524—an increase of $773,240

- A charitable gift of $1.5 million

This plan is basically identical to their current plan until the survivor's death. At that time, the qualified plan assets would be placed in a charitable remainder trust and provide an income of $126,524 to the children for ten years. Under Joe and Evie's current plan, the qualified plan assets—after being reduced by just over $1 million in taxes—would go to the children.

Since the assets are placed in a charitable remainder trust, the $1.5 million would go—at the end of ten years—to their preferred charity. Because there would still be some tax to be paid, specifically $220,000, the amount passed to the children from Evie's personally owned assets would be $780,000, instead of the $1 million under their current plan. That $220,000, however, could be made up by a payment from an irrevocable life insurance trust.

The cost to Joe and Evie would be the cost for life insurance in the irrevocable life insurance trust to replace the $220,000 lost to estate taxes upon Evie's death. The annual premium in this example would be $2,794. If Joe died first and Evie lived out her life expectancy, the total cost for the life insurance would be about $75,000. The result of the change in their plan would be a significant gift of $1.5 million and an increase in benefits to the children of more than three quarters of a million dollars.

12 Managing The Windfall: Having Your Cake and Eating It

Windfalls happen rarely, and when they do, they usually take you completely by surprise, whether it is the result of winning a state lottery, obtaining a signing bonus, or an inheritance. The lack of preparation, however, often means that the benefits from the windfall depart almost as quickly and unexpectedly as they arrived. The challenge is to make sure that doesn't happen.

We are going to visit with an individual who is faced with the need to ensure that the benefits remain as long as possible. His name is Benito Hernandez, and he has just received an NBA signing bonus.

Benito Hernandez

For as long as Benny could remember, he wanted to play basketball. Growing up as he did in the shadow of Madison Square Garden, professional basketball was never far from his thoughts. As fate would have it, he had as much ability to play ball as he had desire to play it.

Benny was the fourth of eight children in his family, growing up in New York City's east Bronx. The time he spent on the gym floor represented an escape from the too-familiar environment of drug pushers, prostitutes, and petty hustlers who preyed on his neighbors and their families.

As a preteen, Benny had learned about the East Bronx Junior Athletic Club, an organization that attempted to provide direction to youngsters growing up in the temptation-laden projects. Through the club, he developed his extraordinary athletic skills and established the contacts that would take him from the city streets to the halls of a New York City university well-known for its basketball team, despite his being an indifferent student.

While at the university, Benny demonstrated his ball-handling and rebounding skills as he led his team to victory after victory in New York's subway league. At the end of four years, Benny left the university with a sheepskin and a contract to play in the Garden. Not only did he have a contract, he had managed to obtain one of the largest signing bonuses given to a rookie that year—$2.5 million.

To almost anyone, $2.5 million is a lot of money; to Benny, who, even at age twenty-five, seldom had much more than lunch money and a subway token in his pocket, it was a blessing beyond belief. After paying income taxes, which left him with about $1.5 million, he knew there were things he had to do for his family and for the East Bronx Junior Athletic Club. After donating $50,000 to the club and moving his family to a single family home on Long Island, he was still left with more than $1 million. Fortunately, while at the university, Benny had been introduced to a financial adviser who worked principally with professional athletes.

Benny met with the planner, who suggested they spend some time talking about what Benny wanted to accomplish and set some goals. After a lengthy data-gathering session, he listed the following goals that Benny had discussed with him:

1. To avoid ever being poor again. Benny had heard of many professional athletes who enjoyed large incomes for a few years only to slip into obscurity with nothing to their name, when their careers faded. He wanted to be sure that would never happen to him. He estimated that his basketball career would probably not exceed fifteen years, and that was only if he were lucky.

2. To provide a $1 million death benefit to his family.

3. To make a substantial gift to the East Bronx Junior Athletic Club and to several charities that had helped him and his family.

The Plan

The financial adviser began the meeting by observing that when professional athletes retire poor, it is usually due to far too many taxes and far too little planning. The plan that Benny would look at resolved both of those problems. According to the plan, Benny would use $1 million to provide a guaranteed income for himself, beginning at the time he retired from professional sports in fifteen years. By the time of Benny's death, which the planner estimated would be at age eighty-four, the $1 million invested would have given him a total income of more than $22.1 million. The plan was flexible enough that the income could be accelerated or delayed, depending upon what made the most sense in Benny's situation. Upon Benny's death, his family would receive $1.5 million. In addition, however, the Benny Hernandez Charitable Family Foundation would receive about $6.7 million—which would be administered by and provide an executive director's income for Benny's future children.

According to the plan, Benny would:

1. Establish two irrevocable trusts: a specially-designed charitable remainder trust that would permit the tax-deferred accumulation of income during his playing years and a wealth replacement trust that would apply for and own a $1.5 million life insurance policy on Benny's life.

2. Name himself as a co-trustee of the charitable remainder trust to maximize his control over the transferred assets.

3. Transfer $1 million to the charitable remainder trust. These funds would be invested in a financial product that would distribute income or not, as the trustees desired. The balance in the trust at Benny's death would pass to the Benny Hernandez Charitable Family Foundation.

4. Be examined for the $1.5 million life insurance policy and withdraw $7,616 each year for fifteen years, to produce $4,600 after tax each year to pay the premium.

INVESTMENT ASSET ANALYSIS

	DIRECT INVESTMENT PLAN	THE CRT PLAN
Bonus available for investment	$1,000,000	$1,000,000
Fund balance in fifteen years*	$4,177,248	$4,049,509
less, income taxes on growth at 39.6%	− 1,258,190	− 0
less, life insurance premium#	− 0	− 114,240
Assets available to produce income	$2,919,058	$3,935,269

* Based on an annual average return of 10 percent net of expenses. Return is not guaranteed.

Amount shown is the gross amount required in a 39.6 percent income tax bracket to pay the annual premium due for fifteen years.

If Benny invested the $1 million in a non-tax-deferred investment—the "direct investment plan" illustrated on the investment asset analysis—he would pay the income taxes as the investment grew in value. However, if he contributed the $1 million to a charitable remainder trust, no taxes would be paid on the earnings since the trust is tax-exempt. As a result, the $1.26 million that the direct investment plan would incur in taxes would be avoided and would provide more assets with which to produce Benny's income when he retired from professional sports. In addition, Benny would receive an income tax deduction of about $110,000, which, in his tax bracket amounted to more than $43,000 in tax savings.

Since the assets in the charitable remainder trust would pass to the family foundation at Benny's death, rather than to his family, Benny's family would receive $1.5 million of tax-free life insurance proceeds to replace the assets they would have received if Benny had not placed them in the charitable trust. The total before-tax income needed to pay the premiums on that life insurance for fifteen years was $114,240, and that was withdrawn from the charitable trust as income. The result is that after fifteen years, the charitable remainder trust assets amount to greater than $1 million—or 35 percent more than the assets contained in the direct investment plan.

INCOME ANALYSIS

	DIRECT INVESTMENT PLAN	THE CRT PLAN
Gross income*	$ 291,906	$ variable
times, income tax rate	× 39.6%	× 39.6%
Income tax#	$ 115,595	$ variable
Gross income#	$ 291,906	$ variable
less, income tax	− 115,595	− variable
Net income	$ 176,311	$ variable
times, life expectancy	× 44	× 44
Lifetime net income	$7,757,684	$13,363,500
plus, income tax savings	+ 0	+ 43,560
Lifetime spendable net income	$7,757,684	$13,407,060

* Based on an annual average return of 10 percent. Return is not guaranteed.

\# Based on a non-guaranteed annual 10 percent return, CRT retirement income begins at $325,000 at age forty and increases to $1,000,000.

Benny's income analysis shows that simply because the $1 million had been put in the charitable trust instead of being put into some investment on which Benny would have to pay taxes, his spendable retirement income would jump by more than $5.6 million.

Instead of receiving $7.8 million, he would receive $13.4 million—an increase of 73 percent. But not only would Benny receive more, his family and the East Bronx Junior Athletic Club would receive over $6.6 million. His family would receive a 14 percent greater inheritance through the charitable remainder trust plan, which amounts to slightly in excess of $186,000 more.

ESTATE ANALYSIS

	DIRECT INVESTMENT PLAN	THE CRT PLAN
Value of the asset	$2,919,058	$6,667,350
less, charitable deduction	— 0	— 6,667,350
Value of the asset in the taxable estate	$2,919,058	$ 0
Value of the asset in the taxable estate	$2,919,058	$ 0
times, the estate tax rate	× 55%	× 55%
Estate tax payable on the asset	1,605,482	$ 0
Value of the asset in the taxable estate	$2,919,058	$ 0
less, the estate tax payable	— 1,605,482	— 0
Value of the asset to Benny's family	$1,313,576	$ 0
plus, life insurance payable to the family	+ 0	+ 1,500,000
Total assets passed to Benny's family	$1,313,576	$1,500,000

There are also some hidden benefits for his family. In every case, the charitable remainder trust plan has resulted in more benefits—73 percent more spendable income for Benny, 14 percent greater inheritance for his family and over $6.6 million for charity. In order to maintain their charitable status, family charitable foundations are required to distribute at least 5 percent of their assets each year. If Benny's family foundation, in any year, had assets of $6,667,350, they would need to give away at least $333,368 to qualified charities. If the assets produced an annual return of just 8 percent, the foundation would earn $533,388. Since $333,368 would need to be distributed, the balance—$200,020— would be available to pay expenses, including the salary for someone to administer the foundation. That administrator could be a family member.

SUMMARY ANALYSIS		
	DIRECT INVESTMENT PLAN	THE CRT PLAN
Benny's lifetime spendable income	$7,757,684	$13,407,060
Lump-sum benefits for the family	$1,313,576	$ 1,500,000
Charitable gift to the family foundation	$ 0	$ 6,667,350

So, in addition to providing a lump sum of $1.5 million to Benny's family at his death, the charitable remainder trust plan would permit him to provide lifetime employment—at a substantial income—for one or more members of his family to administer the foundation that he created.

13 Where Do We Go from Here?

If a man shuts his ears to the cry of the poor,
he too will cry out and not be answered.

—Proverbs 21:13

The Need for Skilled Counsel

We have presented a dozen situations in which the use of a charitable remainder trust would enable our clients to more effectively meet their objectives—to increase income, to preserve the value of assets intact for heirs, to diversify a highly appreciated portfolio, to provide substantial and meaningful charitable gifts to organizations that make a difference in people's life. The clients who were presented are, of course, composites of many clients.

Our intention was to present this incredibly powerful tool for good in a simple, straightforward way so that readers whose background may not be financially oriented could understand it and appreciate its possible application to their life. However, there is always the risk that, in our efforts to simplify, we have painted a picture that inaccurately portrays the complicated nature of this highly technical process and its underlying complexities. If we have done that, we offer a contrite apology and the strongest urging that readers who can relate to any of the case histories and want to learn more seek skilled, qualified counsel—and not attempt to implement these strategies without that kind of counsel. The attempt to do that could prove very costly. I will share a final story that may help to illustrate the value of the skilled financial adviser.

The Kleinmans

Myra and George Kleinman were the owners and senior executives of ValuFresh, a profitable twelve-store grocery chain. As they approached their mid sixties, they looked forward eagerly to retirement. The problem, as they saw it, was the need to sell the business. The growth and profitability of the chain were due principally to the more than forty years of experience they had. If they were to retire and leave the company's management in the hands of others, there was little assurance that its profitability would continue. Over the last few years, they had begun discussions with several potential buyers of the business, only to find that the capital gains tax they would be required to pay was a deal-killer.

They entered into negotiations to sell the company to another small chain and explained to the potential buyer that taxes had stood in the way of previous sales of the company. The buyer told Myra and George that he had heard of a method to avoid having to pay capital gains and income taxes on the sale of appreciated assets and related what he knew about charitable remainder trusts. He suggested that, if they could agree upon a price, they should sign a contract under the terms of which the sellers—as trustees of a charitable remainder trust—would sell the company and the buyer would agree to buy it at that price. Since the charitable trust could sell the company without paying taxes on the gain, Myra and George could have all of the proceeds earning income for them, instead of using some of it to pay taxes. They agreed on the spot to have the contract drawn up to do just that. In fact, their son-in-law, a recent law school graduate, could write the contract and put together the trust.

Over the next two months, the new lawyer drafted the contract to sell the company and copied a sample charitable remainder unitrust for Myra and George's signatures. They executed the documents, naming their favorite charity as the remainderman, and transferred their shares of the business into the charitable remainder trust. The Kleinmans, acting as co-trustees of the trust, sold the company shares to the buyer—in accordance with the contract—and invested the funds to produce income for themselves, happy in the knowledge that their retirement investment would not be reduced by the almost $2 million of capital gains and income taxes that would have been required by an outright sale. Furthermore, they had been able to accomplish it without having to hire expensive planners.

Tax Problems

When the Kleinmans met with their accountant, all of the transactions had been completed, and they wanted him to have the information so that he would be able to take all of the tax benefits to which they were entitled because of the gift. After discussing what they had done with the accountant, they left the records with him, along with copies of the trust and the contract to sell the business, scheduling a follow-up meeting for the following week.

Concerned that his clients chose not to retain skilled counsel before setting up the trust and wanting to be sure of the tax situation, the accountant telephoned a colleague who had been with the IRS for several years, for advice. The accountant related that his clients entered into a charitable remainder trust and transferred their company stock into it, according to the contract. The colleague stopped the accountant and asked him to repeat what he had just said. When he did, the colleague expressed disbelief that nobody had advised the Kleinmans that the prior contract to sell the shares would result in the passing through of the capital gains tax liability to the trust grantor—the Kleinmans.

"Essentially," the colleague began, "the trust acted as the Kleinmans' agent in selling the stock shares." The former IRS agent continued to explain that the agency relationship resulted in the same tax status for the Kleinmans as if they had sold the stock shares themselves. In short, they were responsible for the capital gains taxes of almost $2 million. The accountant called George Kleinman as soon as he had finished speaking with the former IRS agent and suggested they meet immediately to discuss a possible tax problem.

When the accountant had related the substance of his conversation with his colleague to Myra and George, they stared at him in disbelief. The trust was designed to do what it had done. All they did by signing the contract was to ensure that it would happen the way it was supposed to. Finally, George said they would have to take the money out of the trust to pay the taxes.

"It is too bad that the trust didn't work the way it should have," George continued, "but we will just revoke the trust and pay the taxes. We're no worse off than if we had just sold the company as we probably would have done anyway."

The accountant had read the documents the Kleinmans had given him, including the charitable remainder trust, and thought that, although they had the right to act as trustees, he didn't remember they had the right to revoke the trust. He suggested they discuss their options with their attorney. They promised to do that right away.

It didn't take the attorney long to understand what had happened. The Kleinmans had attempted to enter into a complex trust relationship without the guidance that a professional could have provided. The question was just how big a problem that was going to cause. The Kleinmans had explained that the bulk of their assets were comprised of their shares in the business, the proceeds from the sale of which now resided in the trust.

The attorney reviewed the trust document; that would be the key to whether the Kleinmans could revoke the trust and extricate themselves from their tax dilemma. As things stood, the trust would provide Myra and George with $345,143 each year after taxes—enough to allow them to maintain their lifestyle and do some traveling. Not nearly enough to permit them to pay $2 million in taxes! Unfortunately, the trust document—carefully copied from the sample—was perfect. It was irrevocable, and there wasn't even a typo in it. The attorney knew that, even if the trust document had contained a flaw, the remainderman charity would have been likely to initiate a lawsuit if the trust had been revoked. Without a flaw in the document that the attorney could hang his hat on, there was little chance the Kleinmans would be able to change what they had done.

The final result of the Kleinmans' dilemma was that their gift was irrevocable—the gift made to the trust would stay there—and that they owed $2 million in taxes on the gain resulting from the sale. Unfortunately, the IRS held that the taxes were due because the trustee was under a contractual obligation to sell the shares *before* the gift was made, not because the trust or the gift, itself, was invalid. If the gift or trust had been declared invalid, the Kleinmans might have been able to unwind the transaction, pay the taxes from the proceeds of the sale and invest the difference. But, it was not to be.

The Solution

Unfortunately, for the Kleinmans there was no happy solution. The decision to save a planner's fee led to an unfortunate outcome. For the many happy clients that have recognized the value of and employed skilled professional counsel, the pitfalls that plague the unaware—like the Kleinmans—are not a problem.

The first step in dealing with the issues that we have detailed in the preceding chapters is to develop an awareness of the potential problems inherent in the failure to adequately plan, to recognize the situations that can be resolved, and to seek help. That help may come from your attorney, your accountant, or a financial adviser. The key question to pose to your adviser is whether he or she is an expert in the use of charitable approaches to estate and financial planning problems.

Benefits of Using a Charitable Remainder Trust

As we detailed in the earlier chapters, there are many advantages to using a charitable remainder trust. They fall, generally, into two categories: tax advantages and financial planning advantages.

The tax advantages are:

- Obtaining a current income tax deduction

- Avoiding tax liability completely on the sale of appreciated property

- Avoiding estate taxes on selected assets

The financial planning advantages—some of which flow directly out of the tax advantages—are:

- Increased after-tax income to the client

- Increased value of assets transferred to the client's heirs

- Protection of selected assets from creditors

- Creation of an endowment to favorite charities or to the client's family foundation

The net results of the use of a charitable remainder trust for the appropriate client and his or her family are usually a larger current income and a greater inheritance. Not a bad result, especially when you consider that a charity that you choose will receive a large gift *in addition to all of the benefits for the client and his or her family.* In short, for the right client, there is no better way to achieve these benefits. But, who is an appropriate candidate for a charitable remainder trust?

The Appropriate Candidate for a Charitable Remainder Trust

There is no singular appropriate candidate for a charitable remainder trust; there are many, and they have widely varying interests and objectives. The candidates would include people who want to:

- Accumulate assets for retirement and who may have maximized their conventional retirement plans

- Sell an appreciated asset of significant value

- Change an investment strategy that includes the sale or exchange of stocks or bonds that have grown considerably in value

- Retire from and sell a business

- Reduce estate taxes

- Diversify a highly appreciated investment portfolio

- Make a significant charitable gift without adversely affecting their current income or their heirs' inheritance

What to Expect

Although it is convenient and more simple to discuss charitable planning as a separate discipline, the fact is that few clients have lives that are so segmented. What we do in one area of our life has important consequences for the other areas of our life. For that reason, most competent planners will strongly advise a potential client to consider charitable planning as part of a thoroughgoing financial- and estate-planning process. While any financial adviser may deviate somewhat from the process shown below, all good planners recognize that a complete understanding of the client's situation, including objectives, assets, liabilities, etc., is absolutely essential for the development of appropriate strategies. For that reason, an extensive data-gathering interview is always scheduled as a part of the process.

The process normally begins with an exploratory interview, the principal objective of which is to determine if there is sufficient client benefit to be derived from planning.

The First Meeting

During this exploratory session, which is normally at no charge, the adviser will:

- Explain the planning process, including the anticipated number and content of subsequent meetings

- Explain who should be concerned with planning

- Discuss how the tax laws work, including those governing the imposition and extent of income, gift, and estate taxes

- Outline the mistakes that are commonly made because of a lack of proper planning

- Explain the basis and extent of the adviser's compensation for the planning

The competent adviser will candidly share information about his or her approach, credentials, references, and fees. Recognizing that implementing the proper strategies can mean the difference between the client's achieving his or her goals and failing in the attempt, the savvy client will ask any questions of concern and will contact the references the adviser provides. The client will usually be given a financial planning agreement for his or her review and signature, which details the work the adviser has agreed to undertake and the fees that have been agreed upon. But, once the exploratory meeting has concluded and the client has agreed to work with the adviser, what can the client usually expect?

The Data-Gathering Meeting

The most important planning meeting the client will have with the adviser is the meeting devoted to gathering the client's data. Normally, the adviser will have provided an extensive data-collection form to the client at the conclusion of the first meeting and requested that it be completed and returned prior to the second meeting. This data-collection form will ask for the following kinds of information:

- Personal information concerning the client and his or her immediate family, i.e., names, addresses, birth-dates, Social Security numbers, business addresses and telephone numbers, and any special medical or other concerns

- Employment information, including income, duration, and future plans

- Personal information concerning the client's extended family, i.e., parents, siblings, grandchildren, etc., their addresses, ages, telephone numbers, and the likelihood of their eventual or current dependency

- Client advisers, including guardians, executors, accountants, attorneys, banker, trust officer, insurance adviser, investment adviser or broker, and family physicians

- Financial information, including the nature of owned assets, their fair market value, location (in the case of real property), method of acquisition, purchase price (or value at time of inheritance), and ownership arrangements

- Investment income, including rents, royalties, fees, commissions, and trust income

- Mortgages, loans, and other debts

- Insurance coverages, including life insurance (amount, type, beneficiaries, and ownership arrangements), disability insurance, health insurance, and long-term care insurance.

In addition, the client will usually be asked to bring several documents to the data-gathering meeting. The adviser will keep the documents until they have been completely reviewed and their impact on proposed strategies has been assessed. The documents that will normally be requested are:

- Current wills

- Trust documents, i.e., documents created by the client or of which the client is a beneficiary

- Personal income tax returns for the last three years—both state and federal forms

- Gift tax returns for all years

- Business tax returns for the last three years

- Business P&L and balance sheets for last three years

- Existing partnership agreements, corporate minute books, buy/sell agreements, employment contracts, and stock redemption agreements

- Life insurance, health insurance, disability insurance, homeowner, and personal property insurance policies

- Prenuptial or post-nuptial agreements

- Divorce decrees and property settlements

- Real estate deeds

Once the client has provided all of that information and those documents, he or she usually feels that nothing more ought to be needed. This is far from the case. The documents and financial data that have been provided only give the adviser the "hard" facts; these are important, but, by themselves, they provide only a part of the picture. The rest of the picture is provided by the client's particular feelings about things and people, and the goals he or she wants to accomplish. These are determined through an extensive face-to-face data-gathering session, which may take two to three hours or longer.

The goal of this session is to give the adviser enough information about the client, so the adviser can develop alternative strategies that are effective in achieving the client's goals and consistent with the client's values and other goals. For example, an adviser might usually recommend a particular strategy to minimize taxes. However, knowing the client's desire to accomplish other goals, the specific tax-minimizing strategy may be inappropriate. While candor is important in any client-adviser relationship, there is an absolute and overriding need for candor in this data-gathering step.

After the data-gathering meeting, the adviser will inventory the client data and list client goals in the order of their priority. He or she will then analyze the situation for obvious inconsistencies.

The Third Meeting

Since so much is often at stake in this process, it is important that the adviser frequently check back on his or her understanding of the client's situation and goals. This is the function of the third meeting.

In the third meeting, the adviser will usually prepare a written inventory of the client's resources and a prioritized listing of the client's goals. These documents are given to the client to review and amend as necessary. Upon review, the client is normally asked to initial the documents, as amended, indicating that they represent a true, complete, and current picture of the client's goals and resources. It is based on these documents that the adviser's proposed strategies will be built.

After this third meeting, the planner will apply various tools and techniques to the verified data in order to model outcomes. He or she will normally consider how assets are positioned, taxed, and managed and how income is directed, taxed, and protected. Depending upon the complexity of the client's situation and the initial agreement with the client, the adviser may schedule an initial meeting with the client's attorney, accountant, and trust officer. This meeting is never scheduled without the client's knowledge and agreement. The adviser will then formulate and test alternative plans.

The Fourth Meeting

Remembering that planning is anything but a "one size fits all" process, it is in this meeting that the client is normally given his or her first look at a suggested plan that endeavors to satisfy the client's goals. Depending upon the involvement of the client's other advisers, the client's attorney, accountant, and trust officer may also attend this meeting.

During this meeting, the adviser will take several steps. He or she will usually restate the agreed-upon goals and their priority, identify the specific strategy that will most efficiently accomplish the goals, specify the assets and individuals that would be affected, present a numeric illustration of the strategy, and compare it with the current strategy.

The client will be guided through the plan step by step by the adviser and/or the other members of the planning team. The adviser has the responsibility to ensure that the client fully understands the nature of the proposal and any risks to which he or she may be exposed because of the strategy implementation before the plan is approved and implemented.

The client may choose to direct the team to implement the strategy at the end of this meeting, but it is more likely that there will need to be some revision in the suggested plan before implementation. Once any revisions have been made and the client has approved the plan and authorized it, then the implementation can begin.

Plan Implementation

Usually, before the implementation begins, the client is presented with a finalized report (which incorporates the needed revisions and a timetable for implementation) for review and approval. The client then signs the report, indicating his or her approval of the plan and authorization for its implementation.

In the implementation of most plans, there is a need to draft various documents, revise wills and appoint trustees, as well as to redirect assets to trusts, to purchase life insurance, etc. It is often absolutely essential for the proper operation of the plan that specific people do specific things in a particular sequence. The skilled adviser will provide a sequential list of tasks to be accomplished.

It might not be clear why the timing is so important. Let me offer an example that may help. Suppose the strategy calls for the charitable contribution of a $1 million appreciated asset to a charitable remainder trust and its replacement for the heirs by life insurance. The purchase and complete underwriting of the life insurance is the first of the steps that must be accomplished. If the life insurance were not purchased first and, instead, the gifting of the asset were done first and the client subsequently found that he or she could not qualify for the life insurance, the heirs' inheritance would be significantly reduced. The inability of the client to qualify for the life insurance could require that the strategy be revised or scrapped altogether.

It is important that specific people do specific things. Let's return to our life insurance scenario. Before the life insurance is applied for, many tax-wise strategies will call for the creation of a wealth replacement trust to which we have referred many times in preceding chapters. Once the trust is created, the trustee will apply for the life insurance on the client's life, and the client will never have owned the life insurance policy. The result is that the life insurance death benefit will not increase the value of the client's estate or the estate taxes. Alternatively, if the client had applied for the life insurance and subsequently transferred it to the trust, the death benefit proceeds would be included in the client's estate for tax purposes if he or she died within three years of the transfer. To understand the magnitude of this kind of mistake, a $1 million life insurance policy's death benefits, which are considered a part of the taxable estate, could result in an increased estate tax amounting to $550,000.

The adviser would identify the various documents that need to be created, and they would be drafted by the client's attorney or the attorney (if different) on the planning team. Any life insurance that would be needed would be purchased—usually by the trustee—from the team's insurance adviser, and any tax filings would be accomplished by the client's accountant. The client would appoint trustees for the various trusts and would, usually, appoint himself or herself as a co-trustee of any charitable remainder trust.

There are few feelings that are more satisfying than those we enjoy when we have helped another person. The power of tax planning from the heart allows us to help one another while helping ourselves. It may be the best example of "giving until it feels good."

Glossary of Terms and Concepts

It is not unusual to begin reading about something new only to find that you are spending more time looking for the meaning of unknown words and foreign concepts than absorbing the new material. Perhaps you found some of those unfamiliar words and concepts in this book. To make the job of understanding this material easier, you may want to refer to this glossary frequently. It explains those words used most frequently in the book and is offered in three parts: (a) terms common to trusts, (b) terms typically used in estate planning, and (c) terms generally used in finance.

Trust Terms and Concepts

appreciated property. Appreciated property is property that has increased in value since its initial ownership transfer (by purchase, inheritance, etc.) and on which the capital gains tax has not been paid. Because of the income that must be recognized for tax purposes when the property is sold, appreciated property is often the subject of charitable gifts. The charitable deduction is based on the appreciated value rather than the owner's cost basis.

charitable deduction. The amount that may be deducted from your current income for tax purposes due to your making a charitable gift. The charitable deduction for charitable gifts made through a charitable remainder trust is equal to the current value of the property less the present value of the income to the income beneficiary.

charitable lead trust. A charitable lead trust is a type of charitable trust in which the grantor donates property to the trust that pays an income to a charity for a stated period and then transfers the remainder of the trust corpus to a noncharitable remainder beneficiary.

charitable trust. A charitable trust is an irrevocable trust established for a specific charitable purpose. Although the property in the trust, once transferred, cannot be reclaimed by the grantor, the beneficiary can be changed. For example, if you find you have become disenchanted with the original charitable beneficiary, you are permitted to name a different charitable beneficiary.

charitable remainder trust. A charitable trust that operates just opposite of the charitable lead trust. A charitable remainder trust—often referred to as a CRT—pays an income to a noncharitable beneficiary, called an "income beneficiary," and, at the end of the term of the trust, pays the remainder of the trust corpus to a charitable remainder beneficiary. The income beneficiary is often the grantor of the trust. There are fundamentally two types of CRTs: the charitable remainder annuity trust (CRAT) and the charitable remainder unitrust (CRUT).

charitable remainder annuity trust. The charitable remainder annuity trust—referred to as a CRAT—is a charitable trust under which the income beneficiary receives the same amount of income each year, irrespective of the value of the assets in that year, provided the trust has sufficient assets to make the payment. The payout is determined at the outset as a percentage of initial trust assets and does not vary. The minimum income payout is 5 percent but may be, and often is, higher.

charitable remainder unitrust. The charitable remainder unitrust—referred to as a CRUT—differs from the annuity trust in providing for a varying income payout to the income beneficiary. The trust has three distinct formats, referred to as type one, type two, and type three.

- **TYPE ONE**—The type-one charitable remainder unitrust is called the "standard payout option" and provides for an income payout of a stated percentage, fixed at the start, applied to the current trust assets. So, as the trust assets change due to trust income or losses the payout changes. Note that neither the income payout under this option nor the income payout under the charitable remainder annuity trust (CRAT) is limited to the trust's earnings. In fact, the actual payout may exceed trust earnings and may even be made during a period when the trust experiences a loss of assets due to poor investment experience.

- **TYPE TWO**—The type-two charitable remainder unitrust is called the "net income payment option" and provides for an income payout equal to the *lesser* of the stated percentage of trust assets, fixed at the start, and the income earned by the trust. Note that capital gains are not generally considered to be trust income and that income paid to an income beneficiary may not exceed the trust's earnings in that year.

- **TYPE THREE**—The type-three charitable remainder unitrust is called the "net income with makeup option" and provides for an income payout equal to the lesser of the stated percentage of trust assets, fixed at the start, and the income earned by the trust. In any year in which the actual income distributed is less than the initial stated percentage, a deficit will be reflected that will be paid to the income beneficiary when the trust income exceeds the income percentage. This type of trust is known as a "NIMCRUT" and is often used in those situations in which income deferral is an objective. Income paid to an income beneficiary may not exceed the trust's total earnings.

corpus. The principal of the trust.

cost basis. Generally means what the property cost you, plus capital additions and less any depreciation/depletion that you have taken.

co-trustee. A person (real or corporate) who serves with another trustee.

fiduciary. An individual or institution having the duty to act exclusively for the benefit of another. The fundamental duty owed by the fiduciary to the beneficiaries is one of loyalty. A trustee is a fiduciary with respect to the trust beneficiaries.

grantor. The creator of the trust. Also called the *settlor, creator, trustor* or—in the case of a testamentary trust—a *testator.*

income beneficiary. When used in connection with a charitable remainder trust, it is the person or persons who receive income from the trust prior to its termination and the passing of the corpus to the remainder beneficiary.

independent special trustee. When used in connection with a charitable remainder trust, an independent special trustee is a trustee granted exclusive specialized fiduciary powers to (a) value hard-to-value assets such as stock in a close corporation, (b) dispose of contributed assets, and (c) sprinkle income among income recipients.

irrevocable. When used with a trust, *irrevocable* means that the trust, once established, may not be terminated or changed by the grantor and the property reclaimed prior to the trust's termination by its terms. The property is transferred to the trust permanently. This type of trust is usually needed for obtaining important tax benefits.

life interest. A benefit that continues for the life of the person holding the interest, for example, income from a trust.

living trust. A living trust—also called an inter vivos trust—is a trust that is established during the grantor's lifetime and may be revocable or irrevocable.

power of attorney. A legal document that gives another person specified legal authority to act on that person's behalf, including signing checks and similar means of handling money.

private foundation. Also frequently called a "family foundation," it is, essentially, a private charity. Unlike donations to a public charity, which are deductible up to 50 percent of the donor's adjusted gross income, donations to private charities are deductible up to 30 percent of the donor's adjusted gross income. A private foundation, however, permits the donor or the donor's family to maintain ongoing control over the annual charitable distributions and may provide compensated employment for members of the donor's family. A private foundation is required to distribute at least 5 percent of its assets each year.

qualified terminable interest property (QTIP) trust. A trust that provides the surviving spouse with income for life and then passes principal to the designated remaindermen; it may qualify for a marital deduction. If it does, it will be included in the survivor's estate.

remainder beneficiary. When used in connection with a charitable remainder trust, it is the public charity or private charitable foundation that receives the corpus of the charitable remainder trust at its termination. The remainder beneficiary is also referred to as a "remainderman."

revocable. When used with a trust, *revocable* means that the grantor may terminate the trust and reclaim the property. There are usually no tax benefits associated with a revocable trust.

revocable living trust. A revocable written trust to which a person transfers assets and property along with instructions for the trustee to distribute the assets during the grantor's life and following the grantor's death. The trust becomes irrevocable upon the death of the grantor.

testamentary trust. A testamentary trust is a trust created by the last will and testament of the decedent. It becomes both effective and irrevocable upon death.

trust. A trust is a legal entity that represents and effects a split in the ownership of property into two elements: legal title, which is usually held by the trust, and equitable ownership—a way of saying *use*— which is enjoyed by another.

trustee. An individual or institution responsible for carrying out the provisions of a trust document. The trustee manages the trust for the beneficiaries.

wealth replacement trust. An irrevocable life insurance trust (ILIT) established by a donor of property and designed to replace the value for the heirs of the gifted property. It is often used in conjunction with a charitable remainder trust. Since the life insurance is applied for and owned by the irrevocable trust rather than the insured, the death proceeds are usually completely free of any income or estate taxes.

Estate Terms and Concepts

adjusted gross estate. This is an amount calculated by subtracting the following from the gross estate:

- Allowable debts

- Funeral and medical costs

- Administrative expenses.

administrator. An administrator is appointed by the court to settle an estate in the absence of an executor. An administrator would be appointed if the decedent died without a valid will, if the will failed to name an executor, or if the named executor was unable or unwilling to settle the estate.

credit shelter trust. A trust established in the decedent's will by virtue of which the decedent avoids overqualification (and underutilization of the unified credit).

estate. In general terms, an estate (for tax purposes) is comprised of the total of

- All the property owned by an individual at death

- Any property in which the decedent has any incidents of ownership

- Certain property transferred within three years of death.

Also referred to as the "gross estate."

estate tax. A tax imposed by the federal government and several states on a person's right to transfer property at death. This is a graduated tax with a top federal rate of 55 percent.

executor. An executor is named by the estate owner in the will as the one to settle the estate.

incident of ownership. Refers to an element of ownership of a life insurance policy—often minor—as a result of which the entire death benefit proceeds are included in the decedent's estate for tax purposes. For example, an insured would be deemed to have an incident of ownership if he or she gave up all rights to a policy except the right to name a beneficiary or receive dividends, etc.

income in respect of a decedent (IRD). This is income that was earned but not received—either actually or constructively—by a decedent. It is subject to income taxes. An example of IRD would be the earnings in a deferred annuity at the owner's death.

intestate. The term used for someone who dies without a will.

irrevocable life insurance trust. Often referred to as a "wealth replacement trust," it is an irrevocable inter vivos trust designed to apply for and own life insurance. Since the life insurance is not owned by the insured at the time of death, the proceeds are not included in the estate—thereby avoiding estate taxes.

last will and testament. A will. Generally, a written document by virtue of which the testator disposes of his or her property at death. In English common law, real property was disposed of by will and personal property was disposed of by testament. The distinction is no longer appropriate under U.S. law.

marital deduction. A deduction from the taxable estate for property passing at death to a spouse. Under current law, a spouse enjoys an unlimited marital deduction—which means that all property passing to a spouse will avoid federal estate taxes.

stepped up basis. The treatment given to certain property passing at death which "steps-up" the heirs' cost basis to the fair market value of the property at death. The result of this step-up is to avoid income taxes on a subsequent sale of the inherited property. Not all property enjoys this treatment.

taxable estate. An amount determined by subtracting the allowable deductions from the gross estate. This is the amount with which the executor will enter the estate tax table.

testator. The maker of a will.

unified credit. A tax credit to which the estate of every decedent is entitled. It applies directly against the federal estate tax.

Financial Terms and Concepts

capital gains. Gain or profit arising out of the sale or exchange of a capital asset. Capital gains are taxed at the taxpayer's marginal rate, up to the maximum capital gains rate. The current maximum capital gains rate is 20 percent. The use of a charitable remainder trust (CRT) is a popular method of avoiding the income tax payable on capital gains and is the reason why appreciated property is often the subject of a charitable gift to a CRT.

diversification. Technically, the process of reducing risk by forming portfolios of imperfectly correlated assets. Less technically, it is the spreading of one's investments over many investment vehicles, some of which are likely to increase in value at the time when others in the portfolio are likely to decrease in value. Diversification frequently becomes more important as the investor ages; often, however, the investment may have appreciated significantly in value and its sale would result in the recognition of capital gains for income tax purposes. People seeking to diversify their portfolios may find the use of a charitable remainder trust to be economically feasible.

present value. Also called "discounted value." When used in connection with the determination of the value of a remainder gift in a charitable remainder trust, it is the fair market value of the gift less the value of the income interest.

Index

A

Adjusted gross estate, 7–8, 128
Administrative expenses: amount
    allowed for family foundations,
    80, 110–11; and estate taxes, 7
Administrator, defined, 128
Age, and financial well-being,
    xi–xii, xiv
Annuities. *See* Variable annuities
Annuity trusts, 25, 26, 28, 29, 124
Appreciated property: and
    charitable income tax
    deduction, 31–32, 36–37;
    defined, 123; effects of taxes on
    sale proceeds, 3–4, 19–22,
    39–41, 44; and need for special
    independent trustee, 32–33. *See
    also* Business property; Capital
    gains; Capital gains taxes; Stock
    sales
Asset or wealth replacement trusts
    (life insurance trusts), 35,
    42–43, 44–45, 121–22, 127, 129

B

Basis. *See* Cost basis
Beneficiaries, of charitable
    remainder trusts, 18–19, 125, 127
Beneficiary, defined, 18, 125, 127
Benefit summary analyses, 53, 60,
    67, 73, 79, 86, 91
Brewer case study, 48–53
Businesses: CRT plans to eliminate
    tax on sales, 61–73; effects of
    taxes on sales proceeds, 3–4,
    39–40, 41. *See also* Stock sales
Business property, CRT plans to
    eliminate tax on sales, 48–53

C

Capital: amount available for
    investment increased by capital
    gains tax avoidance, 43–44;
    financial vs. social, 12–13;
    social, 46, 55. *See also*
    Investment asset analyses
Capital gains: defined, 38, 130; and
    trust income calculation, 27. *See
    also* Appreciated property

Capital gains taxes: and charitable remainder trusts, 19, 20–21, 38, 40–41, 43–44; effect on sale proceeds, 3–4, 19–22, 40–41, 44; rates, ix

Case studies, 46–47; Brewer, 48–53; Cass, 100–105; Grant, 87–91; Hernandez, 106–11; Kleinman, 112–15; Lerner, 81–86; Lincoln, 53–60; Lyle, 68–73; Pearson, 74–80; Smith, 61–68; Wilbur, 92–98

Cash flow analyses, 52, 57–59, 66, 71–72, 78, 85, 89. *See also* Income analyses

Cass case study, 100–105

Casualty losses, and estate taxes, 8

Causa mortis rule, 16*n*

Charitable estate tax deduction, 8

Charitable gifts: deductibility, 30; effects on heirs, 35; replacing value for heirs, 35, 42–43; tax treatment of, 23–24, 30–32; as voluntary social capital, 13, 46. *See also* Charitable income tax deduction; Charitable remainder trusts

Charitable income tax deduction, 19, 21–22, 23–25, 29; for cash gifts vs. gifts of appreciated property, 31–32; and charitable lead trusts, 34; and charitable remainder trusts, 36–38; defined, 123; for donations to public charities vs. private foundations, 30–32; qualified gifts, 29–30; and trust income rates, 29

Charitable lead trusts, 34, 123–24

Charitable remainder annuity trusts (CRATs). *See* Annuity trusts

Charitable remainder trusts (CRTs), 18–34; annuity trusts vs. unitrusts, 25–29, 124–25; beneficiaries, 18–19, 125, 127; and capital gains tax avoidance, 38, 40–41, 43–44; and charitable income tax deduction, 36–38; defined, 124; and estate tax reduction, 42–43; financial planning advantages, 43–46, 116; income from different types compared, 28; income payment options, 24, 25, 26–29, 124–25; need for skilled counsel in setting up, 111–15; operation and tax benefits, 19–22; potential pitfalls, 112–15; selecting investment vehicle, 33–34; separate trusts for individual heirs, 88; tax advantages, 36–43, 116; testamentary, 88–91; using a special independent trustee, 32–33; value of income and remainder interests, 24–25, 37–38, 130; who may benefit from, 46–47, 116–17. *See also* CRT plans; *specific type of CRT*

Charitable remainder unitrusts (CRUTs). *See* Unitrusts

Charitable trusts: defined, 124. *See also specific type of charitable trust*

Charities: public, vs. private foundations, 30–32, 36–37, 126; tax deduction qualification, 30

Charity, government's role in, 22–23, 34

Common law, 5

Contribution base, 30, 31

Contributions. *See* Charitable gifts

Corpus, defined, 125

Cost basis, 4, 39, 125; stepped up basis, 129
Co-trustee, defined, 125
CRATs. *See* Annuity trusts
Creator. *See* Grantor
Credit shelter trusts, 103, 104, 128
CRT plans: to distribute qualified plan assets, 87–91, 99–105; for diversification of stock portfolios, 53–60, 81–86; to eliminate taxes on sales of businesses, 61–73; to increase retirement income, 48–60, 92–98; for investment of additional spendable income, 92–98; for IRA distribution, 87–91, 99–105; to manage windfalls, 106–11; to reduce estate taxes on substantial estates, 74–80
CRTs. *See* Charitable remainder trusts
CRUTs. *See* unitrusts

D

Death benefits. *See* Life insurance; Life insurance trusts
Death taxes. *See* Estate taxes
Debts, and estate taxes, 7
Dentzer, Susan, xv
Disabled individuals, special needs trusts for, 35
Discounted value. *See* Present value
Diversification, defined, 130
Diversifying appreciated stock portfolios using CRTs, 53–60, 81–86

E

Estate, defined, 128
Estate analyses, 2–3, 45, 52, 59–60, 66–67, 72–73, 78–79, 85–86, 90–91, 97–98, 110
Estate planning: potential pitfalls, 121–22; working with a financial adviser, 117–22
Estate taxes, 5–11; and asset replacement trusts, 35*n*; and charitable remainder trusts, 42–43; credits, 8, 10–11, 129; deductions, 7–8, 129; defined, 128; determining taxable estate, 6–8; effect on inheritance, 1–3, 4; and irrevocable trusts, 16–17; rates, ix, 9; using CRT plans to reduce, 74–80
Executor, defined, 128

F

Family foundations, 126; as remainder beneficiary of CRT, 75–80, 108, 109, 110–11; as source of employment for heirs, 80, 110–11. *See also* Private foundations
Federal payroll, xiii–xiv
Fiduciary, defined, 125
Financial capital, vs. social capital, 12–13
Financial planning: potential pitfalls, 112–15, 121–22; working with a financial adviser, 117–22
Foreign death tax credit, 10
Foundations. *See* Family foundations; Private foundations
Funeral expenses, and estate taxes, 7

G

Gifts, noncharitable: adjusted taxable gifts, 8; and estate taxes, 6–7, 8; to irrevocable trusts, 16; made "in contemplation of death," 6, 16*n*; from parent to child, 30. *See also* Charitable gifts

Gift tax, 42; annual exclusion, 35*n*

Glossary, 123–30

Government benefits: dwindling of, xii–xiii; and special needs trusts, 35

Government's role in charity, 22–23, 34

Grant case study, 87–91

Grantor: defined, 17, 125; rights and duties, 32–33

Gross estate: adjustments to, 7–8; defined, 6–7, 128

H

Hernandez case study, 106–11

I

ILITs (irrevocable life insurance trusts). *See* Life insurance trusts

Incident of ownership, 128

Income: deferring, 28–29; increasing through capital gains tax avoidance, 40–41, 44; investing additional spendable income, 92–98; managing windfalls, 106–11; ordinary, vs. capital gains, 38; from trusts, 24, 25, 26–29, 37–38, 124–25. *See also* Retirement income

Income analyses, 96, 109. *See also* Cash flow analyses

Income beneficiary, 18–19, 125

Income in respect of a decedent, 2, 90, 97; defined, 129

Income interest of CRT, valuing, 24–25

Income tax deductions. *See* Charitable income tax deduction

Income taxes: effect on inheritance, 1–3; effect on investment growth, xvi–xvii; history, xvi; state, effect on property sale proceeds, 20, 41, 44. *See also* Capital gains taxes

Income tax rates: effect of Social Security and Medicare insolvency on, xiv–xvi, xviii; history and likely future trends, xvii–xix; state, ix

Independent special trustee, 32–33, 75, 126

Inheritance: CRT plans to preserve value, 87–91, 99–105; effects of estate taxes on, 1–3, 4. *See also* Estate analyses; Life insurance trusts

Inter vivos trusts (living trusts), 17, 126

Investment asset analyses, 51, 57, 65, 70–71, 77, 84, 108–9

Investment growth, taxed and non-taxed compared, xvi–xvii

IRAs (individual retirement accounts): distribution strategies using CRT plans, 87–91, 99–105; effects of taxes on, 1–3

IRD. *See* Income in respect of a decedent

Irrevocable, defined, 126

Irrevocable life insurance trusts. *See* Life insurance trusts

Irrevocable vs. revocable trusts, 16–17

K

Kleinman case study, 112–15
Kolbert, Elizabeth, xv

L

Last will and testament, defined, 129
Lead trusts, 34, 123–24
Lerner case study, 81–86
Life estate, and estate taxes, 7
Life expectancy, xi–xii, xiv
Life insurance, and estate taxes, 6–7, 16*n*, 121–22, 128
Life insurance trusts (asset or wealth replacement trusts), 35, 42–43, 44–45, 121–22, 127, 129
Life interest, defined, 126
Lincoln case study, 53–60
Living trusts (inter vivos trusts), 17, 126
Lyle case study, 68–73

M

Marital deduction (estate tax), 8, 129
Medicare, xii, xvi, xviii

N

National Performance Review, xiii–xiv
NIMCRUT (Net Income Charitable Remainder Unitrust with Makeup Option), 69, 83, 88, 93

O

Ordinary income, vs. capital gains, 38

P

Payment options for CRT income, 24, 25, 26–29, 124–25
Pearson case study, 74–80
Pension optimal plan, 104–5
Pension plans. *See* Qualified retirement plans
Philanthropy, voluntary vs. involuntary, 13, 46
Power of attorney, 126
Present value, of CRT income and remainder interests, 24–25, 37–38, 130
Primogeniture, 5
Prior transfers tax credit, 10–11
Private foundations: defined, 126; tax consequences of gifts to, 30–32. *See also* Family foundations
Public charities, tax consequences of gifts to, 30–32, 36–37, 126

Q

QTIP (qualified terminable interest property) trust, 126
Qualified retirement plans: distribution strategies using CRT plans, 87–91, 99–105; effects of taxes on, 1–3

R

Real estate, effects of taxes on sale proceeds, 40, 41
Remainder beneficiary, 18, 127
Remainder interest of CRT, valuing, 24–25, 130
Retirement income: CRT plans to increase, 48–60, 92–98. *See also* Cash flow analyses

Retirement plans: distribution strategies using CRT plans, 87–91, 99–105; effects of taxes on, 1–3
Revocable, defined, 127
Revocable living trust, defined, 127
Revocable vs. irrevocable trusts, 16–17

S

Settlor. *See* Grantor
Smith case study, 61–68
Social capital, 12, 13, 46, 55
Social Security, xii; effect of unfunded liability on income tax rates, xiv–xv, xviii
Special independent trustee, 75, 126; reasons to employ, 32–33
Special needs trusts, 35
State death tax credit, 10
State income tax: effects on property sale proceeds, 20, 41, 44; rate used, ix
Stepped up basis, 129
Stock sales: CRT plans to eliminate taxes, 53–60, 61–73, 81–86; potential problems of using CRTs, 112–15
Success tax, 100
Summary analyses. *See* Benefit summary analyses

T

Taxable estate, defined, 129
Taxable gifts, and estate taxes, 8
Taxation, 1–5. *See also* Estate taxes; Income taxes
Tax credits, estate taxes, 8, 10–11, 129

Tax deductions: estate taxes, 7–8, 129. *See also* Charitable income tax deduction
Tax rates: capital gains tax, ix; estate tax, ix, 9; income tax, ix, xiv–xvi, xvii–xix
Tentative tax base of estate, 8
Testamentary trusts, 17, 125, 127; examples of use, 88–91, 100–105. *See also* Credit shelter trusts
Testator, 125, 129. *See also* Grantor
Theft and casualty losses, and estate taxes, 8
Trustee: defined, 17–18, 127; duties and obligations, 32–34. *See also* Independent special trustee
Trust income: calculating present value, 24–25, 37–38; cumulative income from different types compared, 28; defined, 27; payment options, 24, 25, 26–29, 124–25
Trustor. *See* Grantor
Trusts: defined, 127; fundamentals of, 14–18; terms and concepts, 123–27. *See also specific type of trust*

U

Unified credit (estate tax), 8, 10, 128, 129
Uniform Prudent Investor Act, 34
Unitrusts, 24, 25, 29, 124–25; types compared, 26–29, 124–25. *See also* NIMCRUT

V

Variable annuities: as CRT funding, 69, 88, 93; outright vs. CRT purchase, 93, 95–98

W

Wealth or asset replacement trusts
(life insurance trusts), 35,
42–43, 44–45, 121–22, 127, 129
Wilbur case study, 92–98
Will, defined, 129
Windfalls, managing, 106–11